PRAISE FOR AGAINST THE CURRENT

Tyler Sansom has done the impossible. He has written a book that could actually heal the political divide with a sensible and biblical overview of not only how America began, but more importantly, how it began to fracture under the weight of Godly deviation and self-hubris. Can we truly be ONE Nation under God, again? Mr. Sansom makes a great run at the question in this self-reflective treatise. Beware, however, like him, you might just find yourself on the side opposite the one you think you're on! Great news, Sansom offers a tangible way to return to the side of righteousness.

—Daniel Roebuck, Actor, Producer, Director, *Sinner*

***

Lead me in your way, O Lord, and I will walk in your truth; Gladden my heart so as to fear your name. (Psalm 85/86) In a deeply divided world, rife with distraction, Tyler Sansom, expertly illuminates our past and encourages us, regardless of tradition and politics, to focus our hearts toward the narrow gate and walk the path of salvation.

—Demetrios Troy, Actor - *The Chosen*

***

Such a great book—it is so captivating from the beginning to the end. Throughout every chapter of this book Tyler goes through the history of different American events to current American ideals versus what it is like to love Jesus more than the ideals and political parties of this world. He explains through scripture and historical events how much of our past culture isn't so different from what's happening in our world presently. We need to remain focused on loving Jesus and prioritizing him more than loving this world and its trends and Tyler Sansom does an amazing job explaining and showing us that in this book. He explains that setting aside all politics and differences in this world and coming together through Christ and loving Jesus and each other is far more important than any party or trending ideal.

—**Kaleb Ort,** Major League Baseball Pitcher

***

An ever-growing "us vs them" attitude seems to drive more and more headlines, conversations, and political rhetoric, but Tyler Sansom brilliantly illustrates how Christians are called to be disciples before political commentators. A must-read for anyone who's tired of arguing politics, Against the Current reminds us that the Kingdom of God doesn't sway left or right, it calls only for our obedience to our Creator.

—**Justen Overlander**, Producer, *The Chosen*, *The Shift*, *I Can*

***

This book is needed now more than ever. In a time when Christianity is increasingly being defined by political parties rather than the person of Jesus, Against the Current offers a much-needed breath of fresh air. As someone who feels politically homeless and has been deeply perplexed by the shifts in Christian political culture over the past decade, I am grateful for this wise and steady voice. With humility, historical clarity, and deep biblical grounding, the author invites readers to step out of reactionary outrage and cultural panic and back into the steady, life-giving current of Jesus. This is not a call to disengage, but a call to re-center—to ask whether we are being carried by the River of Life or slowly drifting with the currents of power, fear, and national identity.

Especially for ministry leaders navigating deeply polarized spaces, this book provides wisdom, language, and hope. It challenges readers to examine where faith has been fused with fear or control, while also offering practical guidance and tangible steps each of us can take to live with courage, discernment, and faithful presence. Against the Current reminds us that our witness has never depended on political influence, but on our allegiance to Christ—and that the way of Jesus remains not only different, but desperately needed in our world today.

—**Kristy Robison**, President/CEO of *Teach To Transform*

AGAINST *the* CURRENT

Following Jesus In A Nation Adrift

by

TYLER SANSOM

Published by KHARIS PUBLISHING,
an imprint of KHARIS MEDIA LLC.

ISBN-13: 978-1-63746-699-5

ISBN-10: 1-63746-699-4

Library of Congress Control Number: 2026936750

All KHARIS PUBLISHING products are available at special quantity discounts for bulk purchases for sales promotions, premiums, fund-raising, and educational needs. For details, contact:

Kharis Media LLC
Tel: +1 (331) 312-2376
support@kharispublishing.com
www.kharispublishing.com

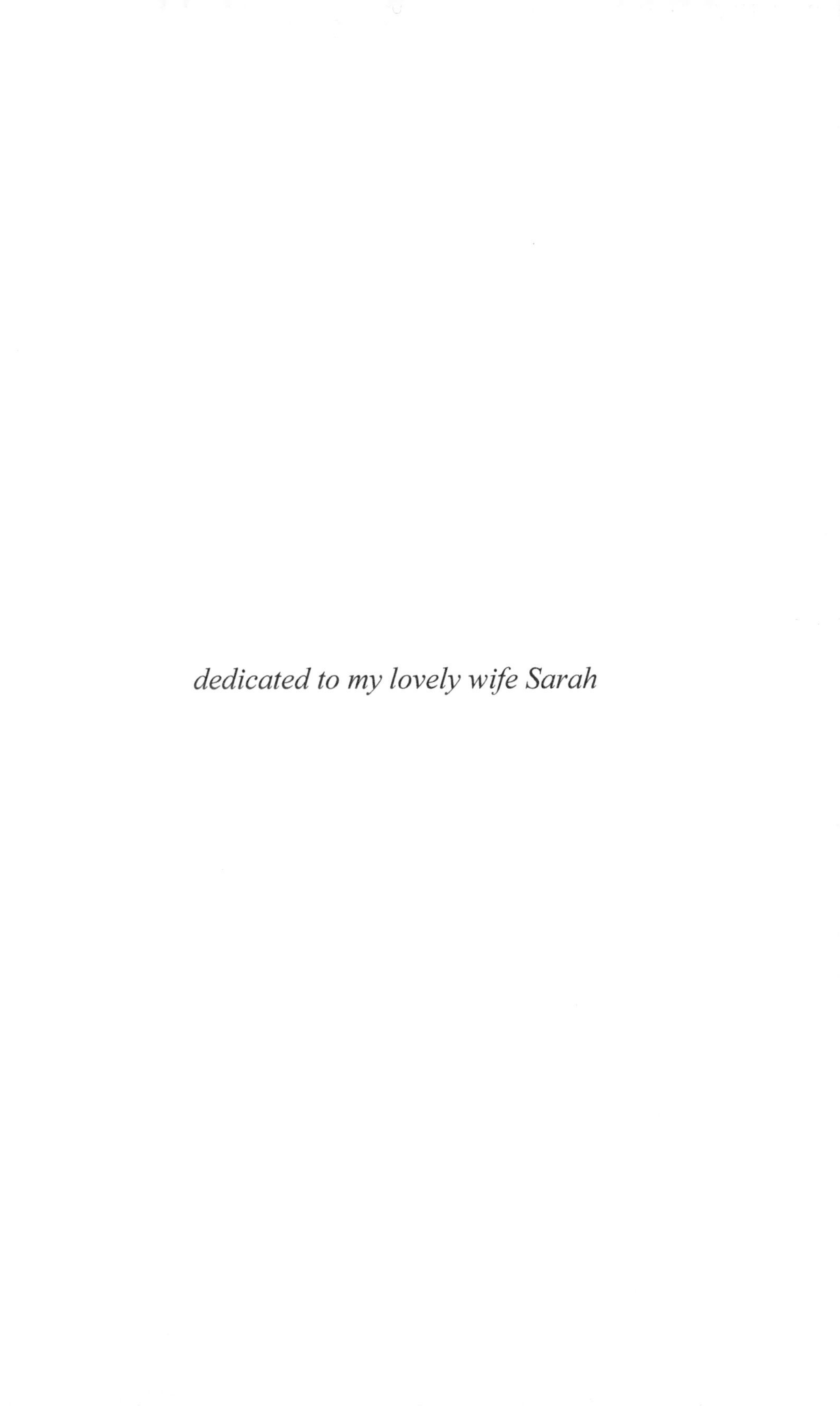

dedicated to my lovely wife Sarah

CONTENTS

FOREWORD

Our church was looking for a worship leader. We found several alternatives, only to be turned down because they were already in position in other major churches. I met up with an old friend to talk about our problems. He listened; then summed it up: "You want a megachurch talent, but you're not a megachurch." He was right! Then he added, "You have to find them before they do." The light bulb came on! I began calling Christian colleges asking, "Who is the best worship leader on your campus." And that's how I met Tyler.

We recognized his musical gift. And we loved his heart. And we offered him a job. Following his interview with our leadership team, Tyler stepped out of the room and one of the men said, "I hope we can keep him 3 years." They recognized his gifts could carry him to bigger things.

But we underestimated Tyler. We saw his heart; we heard his gift in music; but that only scratched the surface. He would convince us to go online with our services when we didn't have the bandwidth in our building to support it. But he figured out a way. He convinced us to try microsites when none of us had ever heard of the term. He took our microsites into jails and prisons and then covid hit and we were uniquely prepared to expand our reach. Church Anywhere was ready to expand into Africa and Asia, and, well, anywhere!

Then he decided we ought to make a movie! What church does that? We don't talk about the first attempt! But we tried. And we learned.

He's produced and directed 3 more so far. Each addresses a social issue—real problems real people face.

Oh, yeah, and Tyler joined the teaching team at the church. And he began to preach. And in 2021 we began the transition for me to retire and Tyler to assume the lead of First Capital Christian Church and Church Anywhere.

Oh, but there's more. He is gifted; we've established that. He's got a phenomenal work ethic; just reading all he's done makes me tired. And he's willing to try things others won't/don't. But there's more. Tyler is more than intelligent; he can think. It's not just retaining facts. Tyler can process. He can connect the dots. He is capable of pulling together facts and creating a picture of our culture. And that brings us to *Against the Current.* For years he has wrestled with what it means to love your country and love God. So, he decided to put his thoughts on paper.

American Christian—is that an oxymoron? Tyler grapples with the question. (I don't want to give away too much, but Tyler and I would agree: There are Jesus followers who reside within the United States—therefore, American Christians.) Now wrestle with this one: "How does a Jesus follower navigate the pull of his national culture?" Does he withdraw? Does he attack? Is compromise the solution? I've wrestled with the same question. So have you that's why you are reading this.

In order to address the question Tyler dives into the last 400 years of our history from the time when Europeans began to cross the Atlantic looking to create a new, better world. They had an idea of what utopia would be. What would they think if they saw what America has become?

He walks through our history, pointing out how the nation grew more powerful, and noting times, places, and people that shifted the direction and speed of the current. But this is not a history book. The centerpiece is our relationship with God and His Word.

The metaphor of running water beginning as a trickle and becoming a powerful current works to show how subtle, yet powerful the pull can become. But the startling piece (spoiler alert!) is that there is not one stream, but two, running side by side: American culture and Christianity. Sometimes they get along, and sometimes they don't. Sometimes they seemingly merge; and sometimes they seem to go their separate ways. This book is for those of us who live with a foot in each. Or do we? Or should we?

We are living in a time when those two currents feel faster, louder, stronger than ever. Voices are louder, politics has grown angrier; people feel permission to act out. In the same moment the church has grown fragmented and confused about navigating the tension between grace and truth. Many believers feel swept along by pressures they didn't choose and currents they can't name. Tyler gives language to what so many have witnessed and felt but struggle to express and process.

Wise men study the past. It can tell us how we got where we are and mistakes we want to avoid. And wise people study God's Word. There are truths, examples, and life principles that guide to the better life God intends for us. Tyler has organized those two streams of thought to bring us to a practical "so where do we go from here?" Expect to have some questions answered. And know that new questions will replace them. What I love about Tyler's work is the application of Scripture to our modern context. He brings the Bible to where we live. That's the way he preaches; and that's the way he writes.

I don't expect you to agree with everything. But I do expect that you will find something that will make you better, and something that will challenge you to walk more closely with Jesus. And that's what we all want, don't we?

I pause to pray that as you read, you will be both steadied and stretched—steadied by the timeless wisdom of Scripture and stretched by an honest examination of the forces pulling on your soul. May God open your eyes to see what you have never noticed before. May clarity replace confusion. May courage replace hesitation. And may you sense the hand of God guiding you.

Take a deep breath. Carry this book into the current with you. Let it sit beside your Bible and your questions. And remember this truth anchors us all: "Greater is He that is in me than he that is in the world."

Now turn the page. The journey upstream begins here.

Randy Kirk,
Former Senior Pastor,
First Capital Christian Church.

Introduction

For most of my adult life, I've wrestled with how to fit my faith inside the boxes that American politics offers. I love America, but I love Jesus more, and that has left me in a strange place occasionally.

When I listen to conservative voices, I resonate with their love for truth and Scripture; roots that have anchored my own faith. Yet sometimes I sense how easily all of us, myself included, can let conviction turn into control, and passion turn into fear.

On the other side, I see compassion and a real hunger for justice yet even there, I recognize the same temptation I face: to value belonging more than obedience, and comfort more than truth.

Somewhere between the two, I've found myself spiritually homeless, loving the Church but uneasy with the tribes that claim to represent it.

If you've ever felt that tension, you're not alone.

I've learned that following Jesus in America often feels like standing between two rivers, both moving fast and both promising to carry you somewhere meaningful.

One is what I call **The Current of Culture**, the ever-shifting flow of politics, media, and public opinion. It can sweep us along before we even realize we're drifting.

The other is **The River of Life**, steady, life-giving, and flowing from a source that never runs dry. It moves slower, deeper, and in an entirely different direction.

This book was born out of my struggle to tell the difference between the two.

For years I tried to wade through the noise to find a faith that wasn't defined by who I voted for or what headline I reposted.

After years of trying to translate my faith into the language of party lines, I finally realized something freeing: the Kingdom of God is not right-wing or left-wing, it's altogether other.

It calls us not to pick a side, but to pick up a cross.

So this isn't a book about politics. It's a book about currents, about the unseen forces that move our hearts, shape our churches, and steer our nation.

It's about how good intentions can become polluted waters, and how the Church can rediscover the clear stream of living faith that still flows from Christ Himself.

I want to be clear: I love this country, its ideals, its creativity, its courage, and the hope it still holds. And like anyone who loves deeply, I carry both gratitude and grief for what it's become.

I believe America has been used by God in extraordinary ways, and that the story of faith here is worth cherishing. That conviction doesn't blind me to her flaws, it deepens my desire for her redemption.

Loving America means wanting Her to live up to her better angels, to return to the justice, mercy, and humility that first stirred her soul.

And that's what this book longs for: not to condemn, but to call us higher. I don't write as a commentator above the fray, but as a follower of Jesus who's been caught in both currents. I've shouted at my TV,

I've scrolled too long, and I've mistaken noise for conviction. But grace keeps calling me back to the deeper water, the place where love drowns fear and truth outlasts opinion.

To understand how we got here, to this divided and disoriented moment, we have to start at the beginning.

We'll go back to the founding of this nation, when two rivers began to run side by side: The River of Life, carrying His presence, purpose, and truth; and the Current of America, carrying ambition, freedom, and fear.

Sometimes those waters ran together and sometimes they clashed.

But by tracing their course, from the colonies to the present, we can begin to see where the currents diverged, and how we might find our way back to the living water again.

This is not just a story about a nation; it's a search for how to follow Jesus in the midst of it. Whether you've voted red, blue, or stopped voting altogether, my hope is that these pages will feel less like a courtroom and more like a conversation.

I'm not writing to argue or persuade; I'm writing to walk with you, shoulder to shoulder in the same waters, listening for His voice together. I am asking us to wrestle with the question: "Which way is The River of Life flowing, and are we still swimming in it?"

Because I believe it's still flowing.

Even now, beneath the noise of our divided age, that river runs, healing, restoring, renewing.

The question isn't whether the river still moves, but whether we've learned to move with it.

That's what this book is about.

Not the noise of a divided nation, but the mercy of a Kingdom, united.

Not clenched fists, but open hands.

An invitation to return, to step into the living water again, and let it carry us somewhere better.

Part

I

THE DRIFT - HOW WE LOST THE CURRENT

*The River of Life has always flowed forward,
healing, restoring, renewing.*

But over time, many in the church in America stopped swimming and started drifting.

*This section tells the story of how the current of faith
that once shaped our nation slowly merged with other streams,
ambition, fear, pride and selfishness, until the water itself began to change color.*

Chapter One

THE RIVER

Every river has a current. It's subtle at first, a gentle pull that carries you downstream without much effort. Culture, like water, always moves somewhere, and if we're not paying attention, it can carry even sincere believers downstream before we realize we've drifted. Slowly, quietly, it moves hearts, ideas, and even churches in directions they never intended to go.

From the beginning, the American story has flowed within that current, a mixture of faith and ambition, freedom and fear. Faith has been both the sail that propelled us forward and the anchor that held us steady, yet sometimes, it's also been the chain that kept us from moving where God wanted us to go. Our nation's faith has inspired courage and compassion, yet, like all human faith, it's also stumbled under the weight of fear and control. It gave us our moral language, our passion for liberty, and our instinct for compassion. But it also became entangled with power, politics, and pride.

To follow Jesus in America has always meant loving our nation deeply, but refusing to let its current carry our hearts away from the Kingdom. That's what this chapter, and really this entire book, is about. What does it mean to be citizens of *The River of Life* in a world that keeps drifting further from the King? How do we reclaim ancient spiritual rhythms in an age addicted to noise and novelty? And how do we love a nation without confusing it for the Kingdom of God? These are not just questions of theology, they're questions of identity.

God has always asked His people to live by a different current. In Leviticus 18, He told Israel not to imitate the nations they'd seen or the one they were entering. Not Egypt behind them, not Canaan before them. Both lands had strong currents of power, sexuality, and religion that promised life but delivered bondage. "You must not live as they do," God said. "Keep My decrees and you will live by them."

At the end of that chapter, He warns that when a people fill the land with corruption, even creation itself rejects them, "the land will vomit you out." Holiness, then, isn't prudish withdrawal; it's alignment with the life-giving rhythm of God. To live differently is to let His river cleanse and renew what the world pollutes. The call that began at Sinai still runs through the Church today: Don't drift with the current, dwell differently so that life can flourish again. Centuries later, God gave Ezekiel a vision of what that life would look like, a river that would make everything it touched come alive.

The prophet Ezekiel once saw a river flowing from the temple, a tiny trickle at first, spilling out from beneath the threshold of God's presence (Ezekiel 47).[1] As the prophet walked with his guide, the water deepened, ankle-deep, then knee-deep, then waist-deep, until it became a river that could not be crossed.[2] Wherever that river went, life flourished. The Dead Sea became fresh. Trees bore fruit every month. What was once barren came alive again.

That's the vision of God's Kingdom, life flowing outward from His presence, transforming everything it touches.

---

[1] *The Holy Bible*, New International Version (Colorado Springs: Biblica, 2011), Ezekiel 47:1–12.

[2] Ibid., Ezekiel 47:3–5.

The angel calls Ezekiel "son of man," a reminder of his mortality, a witness to divine renewal. Centuries later, Jesus would claim that same title and fulfill the vision. He became the true Temple, and from His pierced side flowed living water for the world (John 7:37-39; 19:34).[3]

Ezekiel was the son of man who watched the river. Jesus is the Son of Man who became the river, the source of the Spirit that still brings life to dead places. What Ezekiel saw in vision, Jesus lived in flesh.

And now, something even more profound has happened: that same Spirit lives in us. We are now the temple, the dwelling place of God's presence on earth (1 Corinthians 3:16).[4] The River of Life that once flowed from stone walls now flows through hearts of flesh. The life that once trickled from the temple threshold now pours out from the lives of believers into a dry and thirsty world. The question isn't whether the river is still flowing; it's whether we're letting it flow through us.

So when we talk about "going against the current," it's not just resistance, it's participation. We're not standing still while the current of culture rushes past; we're letting a greater current move through us, *The Current of the Kingdom, The River of Life, the Spirit of Christ.* The river still flows, but now it flows through His people.

Jesus described two roads, one wide and easy, and the other narrow and difficult. The wide path is crowded, filled with people drifting wherever *The Current of Culture* carries them. It feels natural, effortless, and popular. But Jesus warned that this road leads to destruction (Matthew 7:13–14). The narrow path, by contrast, is not a path of ease but of purpose. It's the way of truth, humility, and obedience, and though few find it, it leads to life.

---

[3] Ibid., John 7:37–39; John 19:34.

[4] Ibid., 1 Corinthians 3:16.

Both paths are moving; both have momentum. The difference lies in their destination and their source. One flows with the world's current, *The Current of Culture* where comfort, control, and approval are the goals. The other flows from the throne of God, *The River of Life*, where love, surrender, and holiness are the current.

To walk the narrow path is to choose *The River of Life*, to let His Spirit carry you upstream against the tide of pride and fear. It's not just about resisting the world's pull; it's about being fully immersed in God's presence until His life flows naturally through you into the world around you. The wide river may look powerful, but only *The River of Life* brings healing wherever it flows.

The Current of America began as a trickle of faith mixed with fear: faith that God was calling them to build something new, and fear of the unknown that lay ahead. When the first settlers arrived on America's shores, they didn't just plant crops, they planted convictions. Many were driven by faith, longing to build a community shaped by Scripture.[5] John Winthrop's sermon *A Model of Christian Charity* envisioned their colony as 'a city upon a hill', a noble but fragile vision, imperfectly lived, yet rooted in Scripture's call to faithfulness.[6] A City on a Hill was a public witness meant to show the world what covenant faith looked like.

That image became more than a sermon; it became America's self-concept. The early Current of this country ran through biblical ideals, mercy, stewardship, equality before God, even if imperfectly lived out. The vision was pure, but the execution was flawed, and somewhere between the two, the Current began to bend.

---

[5] Edmund S. Morgan, *The Puritan Dilemma: The Story of John Winthrop* (Boston: Little, Brown and Company, 1958), 9–12.

[6] *The Holy Bible*, NIV, Matthew 5:14–16.

The Puritans and Quakers weren't just founding a society; they were shaping a moral imagination.[7] Their belief that every person bore the image of God laid the groundwork for human rights, education, and civic responsibility. They didn't just build communities, they built conscience.

The headwaters of The Current of Culture are rooted in selfishness, whether in greed, pride, or fear, but the *The River of Life*'s headwater is rooted in submission to His will. So over time, The Current of America widened. And as the river widened, its waters mixed with the mud of ambition and pride. Faith that once fueled conscience began to merge with the waters of commerce, nationalism, and power.

I'm reminded of a phenomenon deep in the heart of the Amazon rainforest, where the dark waters of the Rio Negro and the sandy, tan waters of the Amazon River flow side by side for miles without ever mixing. Locals call it The Meeting of Waters[8]. Though they share the same bed, they remain distinct, one dark as tea, the other bright as clay, divided by unseen differences in temperature, speed, and density. From above, it looks like two worlds trying to coexist in the same current.

America's spiritual life has often looked the same. *The River of Life* and *The Current of Culture* have run side by side for centuries, both flowing through the same land, shaping the same story. At times, faith and culture seem indistinguishable, sharing the same channel. But beneath the surface, their sources and destinies remain different. One flows from the heart of God, the other from the heart of man. One brings life wherever it moves; the other, confusion. The tragedy is not that they exist together, but that the Church has too often forgotten which current it's truly called to follow. Sometimes, the urge to merge the two

---

[7] Perry Miller, *Errand into the Wilderness* (Cambridge, MA: Harvard University Press, 1956), 3–21.

[8] "Meeting of Waters," *Encyclopaedia Britannica*, last modified July 3, 2024, https://www.britannica.com/place/Meeting-of-Waters.

bodies of water together ends up muddying both streams, to a point where they are hard to distinguish.

By the nineteenth century, the same Bible that stirred abolitionists to action was also used to defend slavery.[9] The same pattern still tempts us today, twisting Scripture to defend what we fear losing instead of trusting what God is building. The same churches that produced revival also carried the blind spots of their time. The current had shifted, and what once brought freedom began to justify chains.

Jesus warned that "no one can serve two masters."[10] Yet American Christianity often tried to, pledging loyalty to both Christ and country. The result was a faith that sometimes resembled *The Current of Culture* more than *The River of Life.*

From political movements that promised moral renewal to ministries that turned into celebrity brands, we've watched faith traded for influence again and again.[11] But what we lost in the process was something ancient, the stillness of spiritual depth, the humility of service, the rhythm of prayer and presence. We built brands but forgot to build altars.

When the Church stops resisting The Current of Culture, it starts resembling the riverbank.

The Kingdom of God has never flowed with the tide of empire. From the catacombs of Rome to the revivals of early America, true Christianity has always been a countercurrent. It moves in mercy when the world moves in ambition. It forgives when the world demands

---

[9] Mark A. Noll, America's God: From Jonathan Edwards to Abraham Lincoln (New York: Oxford University Press, 2002), 85–87.

[10] *The Holy Bible*, NIV, Matthew 6:24.

[11] Randall Balmer, Thy Kingdom Come: How the Religious Right Distorts the Faith and Threatens America: An Evangelical's Lament (New York: Basic Books, 2006), 22–25.

revenge. It fasts, prays, and serves in a culture obsessed with self. It builds altars where the world builds stages.

Ezekiel didn't just see a trickle; he was invited to walk deeper. Step by step, measure by measure, he entered the flow of God's life until he could no longer touch the ground. That's the invitation for the Church today. The Spirit never called him to measure the water, only to enter it.

Many of us stay ankle-deep in faith, enough to feel refreshed but not transformed. But the Spirit is calling us to wade deeper, to let *The River of Life* carry us where we cannot go on our own. Shallow faith feels safe, but deep faith is where surrender begins.

Because if the Spirit lives in us, then *The River of Life* is already flowing through us. We are not spectators of the Kingdom; we are conduits of it.

If the river that flows from God's throne runs through our hearts, then it cannot flow in harmony with the polluted streams of culture. To be filled with His Spirit means we must move against every current that competes for our allegiance.

To go against The Current of Culture today means returning to the ancient rhythms that once formed the saints who came before us, prayer that lingers, silence that listens, community that costs something, and a love that refuses to weaponize truth. The early Church Fathers called this the way of formation. They didn't just want to believe in Jesus; they wanted to become like Him.

Our modern moment needs that kind of faith again, not reactive, not politicized, but rooted. Not swept along by trends, but anchored in timeless truth. Rooted faith doesn't shout; it endures. The world chases relevance; the Kingdom calls us to resilience.

To follow Jesus now is to resist the pull of performance, politics, and polarization. Those currents run through every camp, right and left, church and world alike. It's to choose depth over noise, discipline over distraction and holiness over hype. This is not the easy way, but it is the eternal one.

Going against the current means we remember what the first Christians remembered, that the Gospel is not about gaining influence, but losing ourselves in love.

Pastors lead with tears instead of talking points. Not because truth no longer matters, but because love gives it weight. It means churches become sanctuaries, not stages. It means believers measure success not by crowds, but by character. It means remembering that the cross is not a prop, it's a posture.

And it means we take seriously the words of Christ: "My kingdom is not of this world."[12] The Church was never called to fight for cultural dominance, but to live out a radical love that overcomes darkness.

Every great movement of God begins with people who refuse to drift. The early Church changed the Roman Empire not by power, but by presence. The Great Awakenings reshaped America not through politics, but through repentance.[13] They didn't lobby for change, they lived it.

If revival is to come again, it won't start in Washington. It will start in the wilderness, in the quiet spaces where God's people decide to swim upstream. Perhaps the next revival will look less like a rally and more like a return to prayer.

---

[12] *The Holy Bible*, NIV, John 18:36.

[13] George M. Marsden, Fundamentalism and American Culture: The Shaping of Twentieth-Century Evangelicalism 1870–1925, 2nd ed. (New York: Oxford University Press, 2006), 3–5.

To go against The Current of Culture is not to abandon the world, but to love it enough to resist its lies. It's to believe that God still works in the margins, still breathes life into dry bones, and still calls His people to live differently. For believers, standing apart from the current isn't rebellion, it's love in motion.

The Current of Culture will always carry us somewhere, toward comfort, conformity, or control. But *The River of Life* calls us higher. It calls us home.

The question that will haunt this book, and, I hope, guide you through it, is simple but subversive:

Are you drifting with the Current of this world, or swimming against it with Christ, the Son of Man, whose river flows through you? Because only one of those currents leads to life.[14]

🕮 REFLECTION QUESTIONS

1. How does the image of a river help you visualize the influence of culture on our faith and daily life?
2. Tyler writes, "Culture, like water, always moves somewhere." What modern examples show the subtle ways we get "carried downstream" without realizing it?
3. In your own words, what is "The Current of Culture"? What is "The River of Life"? How do you see them interacting today?
4. In Ezekiel 47, the prophet sees water deepening as it flows from the temple. What might the increasing depth of that river symbolize for your own spiritual growth?

[14] *The Holy Bible*, NIV, Ezekiel 47:9 or John 4:14 (for The River of Life imagery).

5. Jesus is described as the true Temple and the source of Living Water (John 7:37–39). How does this truth reshape how you think about your own role as a follower of Christ?

6. What does it mean that "we are now the temple" and that "the river flows through hearts of `flesh"? How could this change the way we think about church, worship, or mission?

7. The chapter compares the Rio Negro and the Amazon River, which run side by side but don't mix. How does this image reflect the relationship between faith and culture in America?

Chapter Two

THE POSTURE OF THE RIVER

Let everyone be quick to listen,
slow to speak, and slow to become angry." (James 1:19)

Before we wade deeper into these waters, I want to pause.

I once sat in an office at church with our former lead pastor, Randy, and a lady who disagreed with something we taught. We pointed her directly to the Scriptures and read them aloud. Her response: "I don't care what the Bible says. My grandaddy taught it this way, and that's the way it is." I've seen the same instinct in myself, clutching what I was taught rather than opening my hands to what God is saying. It's easy to read the Bible for *confirmation* instead of *transformation.*

Many of us approach Scripture from a place of emotion, reading it through our own point of view instead of from a posture of surrender. Posture matters. Before we talk about America, politics, or power, we need to talk about *how* we'll listen: **quick to listen, slow to speak, slow to become angry, and quick to repent.** (James 1:19).

I love Scripture. It has shaped my life, guided my decisions, and corrected my heart more times than I can count. But I also want to begin with an honest confession: I don't have it all figured out.

This book doesn't come from a place of certainty; it comes from a place of seeking. Like the prophets and disciples before us, I'm still learning to listen to God's voice above the noise of culture, and sometimes even above the noise of my own assumptions.

It's easy for pride to sneak into our faith conversations, especially when politics are involved. I've felt it myself. We can assume that because we've prayed, studied, or lived a certain way, we've arrived at the final word on how God sees things. But the truth is, following Jesus requires open hands. The moment we close our fists around our interpretations is the moment the living water stops flowing through us.

So, as you read this book, please don't hear it as a lecture. Hear it as a conversation. A fellow traveler, trying to make sense of the river we're all standing in. I know how easily a book like this could become divisive.

Some of what I say will challenge your assumptions. Some may even frustrate you. But disagreement doesn't have to mean disunity. And seeking unity never asks us to deny truth or excuse harm; it calls us to tell the truth in love. My goal isn't to win an argument; it's to invite you into reflection. The Church grows shallow when it stops asking questions; perhaps depth begins again when we admit we don't know everything.

Wherever you fall on the political spectrum, right, left, or somewhere in between, my heart is to draw us all closer to Jesus.

You don't have to agree with me to keep reading. In fact, I hope you don't agree with everything. I hope this book stretches you, provokes you, and pushes you to seek the heart of God beyond the lines we've drawn.

What if, instead of debating who's right, we sat at the same table and asked what's true? What if, instead of assuming bad faith, we assumed shared humanity? What if, instead of fighting to prove our perspective, we fought to preserve our unity in Christ?

This is not about picking sides, it's about choosing surrender. Because the Kingdom of God doesn't move left or right; it moves down and in, toward humility, repentance, and love.

I have deep respect for people on both sides of the political spectrum. I've sat across tables from pastors who vote differently, worshiped beside believers who see the world through opposite lenses, and learned from both.

What unites us is infinitely greater than what divides us. We may differ on policy, but we all ache for redemption. We may argue over leadership, but we all long for justice. We may interpret Scripture through different experiences, but we all stand in need of grace.

If you're a Democrat, you're welcome here. If you're a Republican, you're welcome here. If you feel politically homeless, you're in good company. This book isn't about defending America's story; it's about rediscovering God's story within it. The Church doesn't need another echo chamber; it needs a sanctuary where truth and love meet again.

I believe Jesus is still forming a people who can live differently—people who listen more than they shout. Who serve more than they post. Who pray more than they panic.

That's the way of the River, the way that flows from the heart of God through every generation and every culture. And before we chart its course through history, I simply want to say this: I'm honored you're here.

I don't want to drag you into my opinions; I want to walk with you toward His truth. So wherever you stand, politically, socially, or spiritually, stay in the current.

Let the living water carry us not to comfort, but to clarity.

Not to pride, but to peace.

Not merely to agreement, but to Jesus.

So, as we step together into the Kingdom's River, let's do so with humility and love. Let's navigate these rapid waters, together.

A Reader's Posture (4 simple practices)

1. Pause before reacting (pray James 1:19).
2. Ask: "What part of this challenges me first?"
3. Name what hurts, but stay at the table.
4. Repent quickly where the Spirit convicts.

Chapter Three

RADICAL OR CONSERVATIVE? THE BIRTH OF A NATION

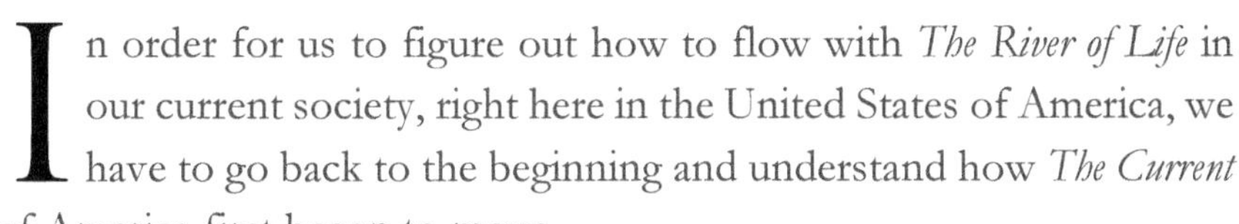

In order for us to figure out how to flow with *The River of Life* in our current society, right here in the United States of America, we have to go back to the beginning and understand how *The Current* of America first began to move.

For our tenth anniversary, my wife Sarah and I went to Boston. A few years earlier, we'd done a surprise trip through a company called "Pack Up and Go." We filled out a survey, handed over our travel dates, and didn't find out where we were going until we got to the airport. Sarah loves vacations. I love history. So naturally, we end up in places like Boston and Philly.

We absolutely loved the opportunity to walk around two of the cities where the United States formed. It was hauntingly beautiful to be able to stand in the church where the Boston Tea Party was first imagined through fiery oratory[15], to see where the Declaration of Independence was signed[16], to see where Nicholas Cage found the treasure map on

15 *Old South Meeting House*, "Boston Tea Party History," accessed October 15, 2025, https://oldsouthmeetinghouse.org/history/boston-tea-party/.

16 *National Archives and Records Administration*, "The Declaration of Independence: A Transcription," July 4, 1776, https://www.archives.gov/founding-docs/declaration-transcript.

the back of the declaration. Well maybe not that one Every brick seemed to hum with the tension between rebellion and reverence.

Our great nation is filled with incredible opportunities to live out history and remember the sacrifices that our forefathers endured. Few places let you walk history like Boston's Freedom Trail[17], a reminder of just how radical the American Revolution was within the grand tapestry of time.

Every revolution begins with a paradox.[18]

To break away from one kingdom, you must first decide what kind of kingdom you'll become. The American Revolution was born in that tension, between the radical and the conservative, the visionary and the cautious, the prophets and the protectors. It wasn't simply rebellion against tyranny; it was a debate about what freedom even meant.

Some saw freedom as liberation, a chance to throw off the chains of monarchy and start anew. Others saw freedom as preservation, a chance to protect timeless truths they believed came from God Himself. Both currents collided in 1776, and the water has been churning ever since. It is nearly impossible to overstate how shocking the American Revolution was to the world.[19] In hindsight, it almost reads like providence. Men with no earthly right to succeed upended an empire. On July 4, 1776, representatives of thirteen small colonies signed a Declaration that would have seemed absurd to any political thinker just a century before: that ordinary men had the right to form their own government, apart from king or crown.[20] This was rebellion against the entire political order of Europe (an age still defined by

[17] *The Freedom Trail Foundation*, "History of the Freedom Trail," accessed October 15, 2025, https://www.thefreedomtrail.org.

[18] Gordon S. Wood, The Radicalism of the American Revolution (New York: Vintage Books, 1993), 3–5.

[19] Bernard Bailyn, *The Ideological Origins of the American Revolution* (Cambridge, MA: Harvard University Press, 1967), 55–58.

[20] The Declaration of Independence, 1776, para. 2.

divine-right monarchies), and it was an ideology that had failed on the few attempts that had been previously tried. It was as if a new creed of freedom was being preached, not from pulpits, but from parchment.

And yet, these men were not anarchists or dreamers. They were wealthy landowners, lawyers, and ministers who feared the chaos of mob rule as much as they feared tyranny. They were cautious visionaries, radical enough to break with monarchy and conservative enough to build safeguards against their own people's passions. From the beginning, the Current of America was a paradox: **freedom birthed in restraint, revolution wrapped in caution.**

Before we go further, we have to understand the philosophical roots that shaped that Current, the Enlightenment.[21]

The Enlightenment (roughly the late 1600s through the 1700s) was a European intellectual and cultural movement that emphasized reason, science, and individual rights over tradition, superstition, and absolute authority. It was an age that taught people to question everything, except the power of reason itself. The Enlightenment gave the world new ways to think about God, power, and humanity:

Philosophy & Ideas: Thinkers like John Locke, Voltaire, Rousseau, Montesquieu, and Immanuel Kant argued for rational inquiry[22], freedom of thought, natural rights, and social contracts as the basis for government; the idea that governments exist by the consent of the governed.

---

21 Peter Gay, The Enlightenment: An Interpretation, Vol. 1: The Rise of Modern Paganism (New York: Knopf, 1966), 5–8.

22 Immanuel Kant, "What Is Enlightenment?" (1784) in *Practical Philosophy*, ed. and trans. Mary J. Gregor (Cambridge: Cambridge University Press, 1996), 11–12; John Locke, *Two Treatises of Government* (London: Awnsham Churchill, 1689), Bk. II, §§ 4–6

Science & Progress: Building on the Scientific Revolution, Enlightenment thinkers promoted observation, experimentation, and logic as ways to understand and improve the world.

Religion & Tolerance: Many challenged the dominance of the church, calling for religious tolerance and separating church from state authority.

Politics & Society: Enlightenment ideas fueled revolutions, encouraged democratic ideals, and promoted education and human rights.

Legacy: It reshaped Western society, laying foundations for modern democracy, human rights, scientific method, and secular thought.

The American Revolution was fueled by Enlightenment thought. Thinkers like John Locke argued that every person possessed "natural rights," life, liberty, and property, and that government existed only to protect them. It was reason echoing Revelation: humans have worth because they bear the divine image. If a government became abusive, the people had the right to alter or abolish it. These thinkers cracked open old certainties like stone, letting reason and inquiry pour through.

The Declaration of Independence echoes Locke word for word[23]:

- "All men are created equal."
- "Endowed by their Creator with certain unalienable Rights."
- "Governments derive their just powers from the consent of the governed."

In those words, you can almost hear Scripture's echo, the Creator granting worth before any government could define it. In that moment, politics sounded almost like preaching.

[23] John Locke, Two Treatises of Government, Bk. II, §§ 123–131; see also Bailyn, Ideological Origins of the American Revolution, 99–102.

These were radical ideas in a world still dominated by kings and emperors[24]. The Declaration was a manifesto of human dignity and divine accountability, an early mixing of The River of Life's ideals and The Current of America's ambition.

Unlike the John Locke from *LOST*, which is one of the greatest TV shows of all time I'll fight you on that, philosopher John Locke was cautious. He saw property rights as sacred and believed order was essential. The Founders, while embracing his liberty, also built in conservative mechanisms to protect against instability.

So the thought process was there, but the war had to be won. The idea was noble, but ideas don't bleed. Men would.

The Revolution unfolded between 1775 and 1783[25], born from years of growing tension between the thirteen colonies and Great Britain. After a series of taxes and restrictions, like the Stamp Act and the Tea Act, colonists pushed back with protests such as the Boston Tea Party. Britain's harsh response, known as the Intolerable Acts, only deepened colonial resolve.

The first shots of war rang out in 1775 at Lexington and Concord, marking the beginning of open conflict.[26] Soon after, the Battle of Bunker Hill proved the colonists could stand their ground against the powerful British army. By July 1776, the colonies took a bold step: the Continental Congress adopted the Declaration of Independence, declaring their separation from Britain and affirming their right to self-rule.

---

[24] Gordon S. Wood, *The Creation of the American Republic, 1776–1787* (Chapel Hill: University of North Carolina Press, 1969), 13–16

[25] David McCullough, *1776* (New York: Simon & Schuster, 2005), 45–47

[26] Paul Revere Heritage Site, "The Battles of Lexington and Concord," accessed October 15, 2025, https://www.nps.gov/mima/learn/historyculture/the-battle-of-lexington-and-concord.htm.

The war pressed on with dramatic highs and lows. Through hunger, snow, and blood, sermons and psalms still echoed through camps. Even in revolution, faith marched beside fear. In 1777, the American victory at Saratoga became a turning point[27], convincing France to openly join the war effort as an ally. During the brutal winter at Valley Forge, General George Washington's army endured incredible hardship but emerged stronger after being drilled by Baron von Steuben. The snow froze their feet, but not their faith. As fighting shifted south, American forces and militias won crucial battles like Cowpens, steadily wearing down the British.

The final decisive moment came in 1781 at Yorktown, where Washington, with French support, trapped General Cornwallis and forced his surrender. Two years later, the Treaty of Paris was signed in 1783[28], officially recognizing the United States as an independent nation.

What began as scattered protests had become a full-fledged revolution, one that reshaped the political landscape of the world and gave birth to a new nation built on the ideals of liberty and self-government.

After independence was won, the real test came: how do you govern? This was hilariously sang in Hamilton by King George when he sand "what comes next?"

That lyric could serve as the theme for the new Republic, a people suddenly free, but unsure how to stay that way. King George's mockery holds a truth that echoes today: freedom is easy to win, but hard to steward.

Consider how conservative the system was by design:

---

[27] Carol Berkin, *A Brilliant Solution: Inventing the American Constitution* (New York: Harcourt, 2002), 14–16; also "Battles of Saratoga," *Encyclopaedia Britannica*, accessed October 15, 2025.

[28] *Treaty of Paris*, 1783, U.S. Treaty Series No. 80, Article I

- The **Articles of Confederation** (1781) leaned too far toward liberty[29]. Each state held most of the power, and the national government was too weak to hold the Union together.
- The **Constitution of 1787** corrected this[30], creating a stronger federal government, but carefully divided it into three branches.

Even liberty needed limits, or so they believed.

- The **Senate** was originally appointed by state legislatures, not voters.
- The **Electoral College** shielded presidential elections from direct democracy.
- The **Supreme Court** was unelected and served for life.

This wasn't accidental, it was deliberate restraint. The Current of America was shaped by two impulses: radical liberty and cautious order.

Though the Constitution never mentions God, the culture of the colonies was steeped in Christianity. Ministers preached fiery sermons declaring Britain a "new Pharaoh" and America a "new Israel." The language of covenant shaped how many colonists understood their rebellion, as a divine mission to establish a free people under God's watch.

Yet the Founders drew a sharp line: no established church. In Article VI they wrote, *No religious test shall ever be required as a qualification to any office*[31]*.*" This was stunning in a world where religion and government were almost always intertwined. America was born not of one current

---

[29] Articles of Confederation, 1781, Articles II–III
[30] The Constitution of the United States, Preamble and Article I.
[31] Ibid., Article VI

but two, the radical surge of liberty and the conservative undertow of control.

- **Radical:** separating church and state.
- **Conservative:** grounding morality in biblical ideas like justice, order, and human dignity.

Now, I have to talk about the elephant or the donkey, I guess. in the room. This is something that has always been a point of mental contention for me.

For all their talk of liberty, the Founders compromised with slavery. The Current of ideals hit the rocks of hypocrisy, and the current split. In those compromises, the moral fault line of America was drawn. Jefferson penned the words "all men are created equal" while owning over 600 human beings in his lifetime[32]. Southern delegates refused to join the Union unless slavery was protected, so the Constitution enshrined compromises like the Three-Fifths Clause[33]. If you don't know what that is, watch the West Wing episode called "Mr. Willis of Ohio," and you can thank me later.

This was where The Current of America clashed hardest with The River of Life. In this casé, conservatism sometimes drifted from preserving what was good to protecting what was familiar or beneficial. It revealed the limits of the Revolution's moral imagination.

The contradiction of slavery shows why America's founding cannot be labeled simply "Christian" or "conservative." Christianity proclaims freedom and the dignity of every person, yet Christians themselves justified bondage. Conservatism defends order and stability, yet at the

---

[32] Henry Wiencek, Master of the Mountain: Thomas Jefferson and His Slaves (New York: Farrar, Straus and Giroux, 2012), 22–24.

[33] *U.S. Constitution*, Article I, Section 2, Clause 3; see also David Waldstreicher, *Slavery s Constitution: From Revolution to Ratification* (New York: Hill and Wang, 2009), 54–58

cost of justice. When faith defends what it's meant to redeem, the Gospel loses some of its living power.

The era was a chorus of conflicting convictions. Thomas Paine thundered for liberty. Adams warned against chaos. Hamilton distrusted the masses[34]. Jefferson dreamed of freedom, even as he owned slaves.

Together, they forged a nation that was neither wholly conservative nor wholly radical, but forever wrestling between the two. Their diversity of thought shows that "the Founders" were never monolithic. The United States was stitched together from conflicting visions[35].

So was America founded on conservative beliefs? The truth is: both and neither.

- **Radical:** It rejected monarchy, embraced Enlightenment ideals, and birthed the first large-scale republic in modern history.
- **Conservative:** It built cautious safeguards, preserved existing hierarchies, and compromised with injustice to keep stability.

In this paradox, The Current of America was formed. It was a nation that aspired to liberty yet clung to restraint, proclaimed equality yet denied it too many people, made in God's image, yet marred by human compromise.

Understanding this tension is crucial for Christians in modern America. When people say "America was founded on conservative Christian values," they compress centuries of complexity into a slogan. The reality is far more complex: America was born from both *The River of*

---

[34] Thomas Paine, *Common Sense* (Philadelphia: 1776); John Adams, *Thoughts on Government* (1776); Alexander Hamilton, *The Federalist No. 1* (New York: 1787)

[35] Mark A. Noll, America's God: From Jonathan Edwards to Abraham Lincoln (New York: Oxford University Press, 2002), 32–34

Life's influence and *The Current* of human ambition, shaped by Christian moral influence but not built as a Christian state.[36]

That complexity matters because it warns us against oversimplification. If we claim America was purely conservative or purely Christian at its founding, we risk baptizing political ideology as gospel truth.

In fact, Augustine (a highly influential theologian) faced a similar struggle in his own life. Before his conversion, he was drawn to the religion of Manichaeism, which taught that the universe was locked in a cosmic war between two equal forces, light and darkness. It is like Star Wars. It was simple, clean, and absolute. But when Augustine encountered the gospel, he realized that this worldview was a distortion of truth. Evil, he came to see, was not an equal power opposing good; it was the absence of good, a corruption of what God made beautiful. The world was not divided into two camps, it was one creation, broken and in need of grace.[37]

That same dualistic impulse still lives in us today. We want clarity without tension, righteousness without humility. But the gospel calls us into a more difficult, more redemptive space, the space where truth and grace coexist.

This is an area of our modern world where we have regressed. No longer, can anything operate within the grey areas. Society wants everything to be black or white. This results in oversimplification of important issues, "us vs them" mentalities, and a pursuit of biased truth rather than actual truth. No longer, are we able to allow two things to be true at the same time. For example, here are two true statements "America was founded with a high influence from Puritan Christian beliefs" and "America's founding was progressive for the time

---

36 Mark A. Noll, America's God: From Jonathan Edwards to Abraham Lincoln (New York: Oxford University Press, 2002), 390–392.

37 Augustine, *Confessions*, trans. Henry Chadwick (Oxford: Oxford University Press, 1991), VII.12–16.

period[38]." Both of those statements are true, but in our modern world, we have a hard time reconciling the word "progressive" with the word "Christian." And that's not just a cultural problem, it's a spiritual one.

The River of Life calls us to live in the tension, to love truth and grace at the same time. The question for us today is not simply what the Founders believed, but whether we are willing to ground our own faith and politics in Christ rather than in selective readings of history.

The revolution was radical enough to start a nation, and conservative enough to keep us clinging to our idols. But *The River of Life* is neither. It doesn't seek to preserve or overthrow, it seeks to redeem[39]. And redemption always flows against *The Current of Culture.*

🕮 Reflection Questions

1. What strikes you more about the Founders: their radical courage or their conservative caution?

2. How do you reconcile America's proclamation of liberty with its acceptance of slavery?

3. Why do you think Christians today often long for a "Christian nation" narrative? Is it historical reality, or a desire for cultural security?

---

[38] Alan Taylor, American Revolutions: A Continental History, 1750–1804 (New York: W. W. Norton & Company, 2016), 411–413

[39] *The Holy Bible*, NIV, Romans 12:2 and Matthew 6:10

Chapter Four

CHRISTIANITY AND THE EARLY REPUBLIC

When the last musket fired and the ink dried on the Declaration, a new question rose over the newborn republic:

Now that we are free, who will we become?

For the first time in history, a modern nation was attempting to build itself not on monarchy or hierarchy, but on morality shaped in no small part by Scripture. And for many of the Founders, that morality was still shaped by the Bible. The young republic spoke the language of faith even as it wrestled with its meaning. Churches overflowed. Sermons shaped public virtue. Prayers opened sessions of Congress. God was everywhere in our vocabulary, but not always obeyed in our practice.

When the Constitution was ratified in 1788, something unprecedented had happened[40]: for the first time in Western history, a nation had chosen to separate church and state at the federal level. This re-charted the national stream: the decision wasn't a rejection of faith, it was a recalibration of it within The Current of America..

40 *The Constitution of the United States*, ratified 1788, Article VI; see also the Preamble.

To understand that decision, we need to rewind about 1,400 years, to a battlefield and a vision that changed the world.

As civil war tore Rome apart, Constantine marched toward its gates[41]. On the eve of battle, legend says he saw a cross of light in the sky with the words "In this sign, conquer.[42]" It was a vision that would blur the line between devotion and domination for centuries. Whether divine or political, this moment marked a turning point: Constantine adopted Christianity (at least outwardly) and claimed the Christian God as his protector.

With victory at the Milvian Bridge, Constantine's rise was secured. He used his new-found Christian identity as both shield and banner, giving Christians reason to hope that their persecuted faith might find favor instead of condemnation. The persecuted church now had power, and power would test its purity.

In 313, Constantine joined forces with Licinius[43] to issue the Edict of Milan, granting legal protection to Christians and ordering the return of confiscated church property. This edict did not make Christianity the only legal religion, all religions were permitted, but it was one of history's great reversals, the persecuted church becoming the empire's chosen faith.

Over the years, Constantine showered the Christian Church with imperial favor: He built basilicas; granted clergy tax privileges, elevated Christians to high office, and draped imperial banners with the cross. He also took on a mediator's role in theological disputes. In 325, he

---

[41] Eusebius of Caesarea, *Life of Constantine*, Bk. I, Ch. 28 (New York: Christian Classics Ethereal Library, 1890 trans.), 53–54.

[42] Eusebius of Caesarea, *Ecclesiastical History* and *Life of Constantine*, Bk. I, Ch. 28–32; Lactantius, *On the Deaths of the Persecutors* (313 CE), Ch. 44

[43]" Edict of Milan" (313 CE), in Henry Bettenson and Chris Maunder, eds., *Documents of the Christian Church*, 3rd ed. (Oxford: Oxford University Press, 1999), 22–23

convened the First Council of Nicaea[44], presiding (or intervening) in debates over the nature of Christ and seeking doctrinal unity.

Though pagan practices remained legal, over time temples lost patronage, and many were closed or repurposed due to lack of support. Constantine's policies, cultural shifts, and his prestige together nudged the empire toward a Christian future. What began as tolerance slowly swelled into triumphalism, a political tide that looked like faith, even when it wasn't *The River of Life*. Constantine never formally declared Christianity the official religion of Rome.

That distinction would come several decades later, under Emperor Theodosius I (380 CE)[45], with the Edict of Thessalonica, which made Nicene Christianity the state church and condemned other Christian creeds as heresy. Where Constantine offered tolerance, Theodosius enforced orthodoxy. Faith gained prestige but lost innocence.

Yet Constantine's reign laid deep foundations. The Christian Church became deeply intertwined with imperial power. *The Current* of Empire and the life of the Church flowed together, often uneasily. Bishops gained political clout; church councils could make empire-wide decisions; Christian festivals, holidays, and moral codes began to shape public law and culture. In the decades following Constantine's reign, Christianity shed much of its earlier marginal status and gradually became the cultural and spiritual axis of the empire. Converts among elites and commoners multiplied, drawn in part by the faith's newfound legitimacy and imperial backing.

Yet this transformation came with tensions. The Church wrestled with internal divisions, often requiring imperial intervention to settle. The blending of church and imperial power also meant that political

[44]" Canons of the First Council of Nicaea (325 CE)," in *Nicene and Post-Nicene Fathers*, 2nd Series, vol. 14 (Grand Rapids: Eerdmans, 1956), 1–3

[45]" Edict of Thessalonica (380 CE)," in Bettenson and Maunder, *Documents of the Christian Church*, 24–25

objectives sometimes shaped doctrine and that dissent could be punished as heresy.

In binding church and state together, Constantine, and those who followed, forever altered the course of Europe [46], ushering in a civilization where Christian doctrine was a pillar of law, identity, and authority. A new pattern set in: state-favored religion as a dominant cultural current

So from that point forward, Europe had a long history of tying faith to political power. England had the Anglican Church. France had Catholicism as its cultural backbone. Even small nations like Sweden or Denmark officially endorsed state churches. Religion and government were fused, for better or worse, and often for both.

America broke the pattern. That break wasn't just political; it was spiritual. The Church would stand, again, in The River of Life without imperial scaffolding. For the first time since Constantine, the Church would walk without imperial crutches.

Article VI of the Constitution declared, "No religious Test shall ever be required[47] as a Qualification to any Office or public Trust under the United States." In one breath, America separated church from state, and faith from coercion. And the First Amendment soon followed: "Congress shall make no law respecting an establishment of religion, or prohibiting the free exercise thereof."

This was radical liberty. But it didn't mean religion disappeared from public life. Far from it. Christianity remained deeply embedded in the nation's cultural fabric. Which leads us to a truth: when the Church practices the way of Jesus, *The River of Life* influences the land without needing to control it. If the Constitution was secular in form, the

---

46 Peter Brown, The Rise of Western Christendom: Triumph and Diversity, AD 200–1000, 2nd ed. (Oxford: Blackwell, 2003), 70–74

47 The Constitution of the United States, Article VI; The First Amendment (1791)

people were not. Colonial America had been shaped by the Great Awakening, revivals led by preachers like George Whitefield and Jonathan Edwards[48] in the mid-1700s. These revivals emphasized personal conversion, heartfelt faith, and moral transformation. The ink on the Constitution was barely dry, but the fire of revival still burned hot.

I will never forget being in 9th grade English class when Mrs. Gensler made us listen to a dramatic reading of a Jonathan Edwards sermon called "Sinners in the Hands of an Angry God.[49]" It was terrifying, and an important piece of literature in American history. That terror, holy, awakening, raw, would soon sweep a continent.

When Jonathan Edwards delivered "Sinners in the Hands of an Angry God" in 1741, he was addressing a colonial audience still under British rule. His words struck like lightning in the dry fields of spiritual complacency. By the time independence arrived, America's heart was already soft from revival.

The sermon's immediate effect was revival, but its long-term consequences stretched far beyond the Great Awakening.

By the time the colonies fought and won independence (1776–1783), Edwards himself had passed (1758), but his sermon and the Great Awakening ethos lived on. America was forming a new national identity, and Edwards 'vision of human beings living under the direct sovereignty of God resonated with the revolutionary spirit in several ways: The preaching style pioneered in the Awakening, intense, personal, urgent, became the template for the new republic's religious

48 Mark A. Noll, A History of Christianity in the United States and Canada (Grand Rapids: Eerdmans, 1992), 88–92; Harry S. Stout, The Divine Drummer: Jonathan Edwards and the Great Awakening (Grand Rapids: Eerdmans, 1991), 45–50

49 Jonathan Edwards, "Sinners in the Hands of an Angry God" (1741), in *The Works of Jonathan Edwards*, vol. 2 (New Haven: Yale University Press, 1959), 57–64

culture.[50] Post-Revolution, revivalists carried Edwards 'legacy into the frontier, where sermons on God's judgment and mercy fueled what became the Second Great Awakening (early 1800s). Out on the frontier, The River of Life flooded dry ground.

Edwards 'sermon pressed the idea that every individual must make a personal decision before God. This meshed with post-Revolution ideals of individual liberty and responsibility. Just as citizens were accountable in a democracy, so too were they accountable before God. This reinforced a culture of moral seriousness in the new republic. The Current of America met the conscience of the Kingdom.

The sermon's vivid imagery of danger balanced with the possibility of redemption shaped American preaching for decades. Post-Revolution America, uncertain about its future, found in Edwards 'framework a way to speak about collective destiny: a nation could prosper under God's blessing or fall under His wrath.

Edwards' sermon became a cornerstone of American rhetoric. Even now, our pulpits, and our politics, still echo Edwards' thunder. In the new republic, schools used it to teach persuasion and moral instruction, embedding revivalist tones in civic life. Even our modern preachers echo Edwards, though often with less gravity and more sentiment.

The post-Revolution generation carried revival preaching into reform movements, abolitionism, temperance, and women's rights. Revival always leaks into reform. The moral urgency of Edwards' style gave activists a way to argue that societal sins were just as damning as personal ones. But revival that forgets repentance becomes activism without anchor. Americans began to see themselves as a people chosen for a divine purpose, echoing Edwards 'warnings and hopes. The same imagery of "dangling over judgment" could be applied to the fate of a

---

[50] Noll, A History of Christianity in the United States and Canada, 94–96.

nation that turns away from God: a chosen people, a divine purpose, and a fragile humility—often forgotten.

While "Sinners in the Hands of an Angry God" began as a local sermon in Connecticut, it planted seeds that blossomed into a defining feature of American spirituality: revivalist, urgent, deeply moral, and infused with a sense of national destiny. Post-Revolution America carried forward Edwards' central idea, that God's hand alone sustains both individuals and nations, and that repentance is the only path to survival and flourishing.

In a real sense, Edwards' sermon gave post-Revolution America not just a religious revival but a moral compass, one that would guide its people through the turbulence of a new democracy.

By the dawn of independence, faith wasn't just preached; it was practiced in every public rhythm. Sermons were political events, often drawing larger crowds than town meetings.

Many states still had religious requirements for office at the local level, even if the federal government did not.

Biblical imagery saturated the language of liberty: colonists called themselves a "new Israel" delivered from a tyrant "Pharaoh" in London.

The young nation may not have had a state church, but it had a Christian moral vocabulary that shaped how people thought about freedom, justice, and virtue.

However, the religious beliefs of the founders varied. Their unity was political, but their faith was personal, and often conflicted.

George Washington spoke often of Providence and God's guiding hand, though he was reticent about his personal faith.

John Adams was deeply moral, but leaned toward Unitarian views of God.

Thomas Jefferson admired Jesus 'moral teachings but rejected miracles, producing his own cut-down "Jefferson Bible."

James Madison strongly defended religious liberty, influenced by Baptist pleas in Virginia.

Together they represented the paradox of America's faith, publicly devout, privately diverse.

Despite differences, most of them agreed on this: faith was necessary for morality, and morality was necessary for liberty. John Adams famously said, "Our Constitution was made only for a moral and religious People. It is wholly inadequate to the government of any other.[51]" Adams saw what every empire forgets: freedom cannot survive without virtue.

This conviction shows the paradox: *The Current* of America ran beside the banks watered by The River of Life, sometimes fed by it, sometimes merely borrowing its language.

In the first decades after independence, Christianity thrived in surprising ways:

The Second Great Awakening (early 1800s) spread revival across frontier towns[52]. Circuit-riding preachers like Francis Asbury brought faith to the expanding west.[53] New denominations flourished, Methodists, Baptists, and others who emphasized accessible preaching

---

[51] John Adams to the Officers of the First Brigade of the Third Division of the Militia of Massachusetts, October 11, 1798, in *The Works of John Adams*, ed. Charles Francis Adams, vol. 9 (Boston: Little, Brown, and Company, 1854), 229.

[52] Nathan O. Hatch, *The Democratization of American Christianity* (New Haven: Yale University Press, 1989), 3–7

[53] John Wigger, American Saint: Francis Asbury and the Methodist Movement (New York: Oxford University Press, 2009), 102–104

and personal conversion. Churches became centers of community life, influencing everything from education to social reform. Christianity was not legally mandated, but it was culturally dominant. Alexis de Tocqueville, the French observer who visited America in the 1830s, marveled at how religion flourished precisely because it was free from government control.[54] Liberty didn't weaken faith, it purified it. Maybe that's why forced faith never lasts, but free faith changes the world.

Faith quickly fueled reform movements: Abolitionists grounded their call to end slavery in the belief that all people were created in God's image.[55] Temperance advocates sought to reduce alcoholism, appealing to biblical calls for self-control. Early women's rights leaders often emerged from Christian reform networks. Each cause, at its core, was a sermon about justice.

In each case, Christianity was a moral engine, pushing the nation to live closer to its founding ideals.

Yet, Christianity also justified injustice:

- Southern pastors defended slavery as biblical, twisting Scripture to serve economic interests.[56]
- Some churches resisted reform, protecting comfort more than truth.

This dual role, prophetic and complicit, shows Christianity's complicated relationship with America's development. Sometimes the Church flowed with *The River of Life*; other times it drifted with *The Current of Culture*. It's the same paradox that still haunts us today.

---

54 Alexis de Tocqueville, *Democracy in America*, vol. 1 (New York: Vintage Classics, 1990), 282–285.

55 Albert J. Raboteau, Slave Religion: The "Invisible Institution" in the Antebellum South (New York: Oxford University Press, 1978), 213–216

56 Mark A. Noll, *The Civil War as a Theological Crisis* (Chapel Hill: University of North Carolina Press, 2006), 32–36.

It's easy for us to bend Scripture toward our preferences rather than let it bend us toward Christ.

Let me give you an example of how this works regarding slavery, the very issue with which the early American leaders had to wrestle.

But the same pulpits that thundered revival sometimes whispered compromise.

Slaveholders in early America often twisted Scripture to justify their practices. They cited passages like Ephesians 6:5[57] ("Slaves, obey your earthly masters") or misused the so-called "curse of Ham" in Genesis 9:25–27 to claim that slavery was divinely sanctioned. By isolating these verses from their context, they ignored the greater biblical witness of liberation, justice, and human dignity. In effect, they bent God's Word to prop up an unjust system for personal gain.

They didn't just twist words, they chained truth.

Yet abolitionists read the very same Bible and found the opposite message. The same book that was used to chain people was also used to set them free. They pointed to Genesis 1:27, where every human is created in God's image[58]; to the Exodus story, where God hears the cry of the oppressed and leads them to freedom; and to Galatians 3:28, which proclaims that in Christ there is "neither slave nor free." They highlighted Paul's appeal to Philemon to welcome Onesimus "no longer as a slave, but as a beloved brother," and they emphasized Jesus' own words in the Golden Rule: "Do unto others as you would have them do unto you." Far from endorsing slavery, Scripture's arc points to liberation, equality, and brotherhood in Christ.

---

57 *The Holy Bible*, New International Version (Colorado Springs: Biblica, 2011), Ephesians 6:5; Genesis 9:25–27.

58 Ibid., Genesis 1:27; Exodus 3:7–8; Galatians 3:28; Philemon 1:16; Luke 6:31.

One faith; two readings—one to oppress, one to set free. I'm more convinced than ever that we can weaponize the Bible so easily we forget how wrong it is to do so.

By the early 1800s, America had developed what scholars call a civil religion[59]: a set of public rituals and symbols that tied faith to national identity. A kind of civic spirituality that blessed the nation without necessarily transforming it. Presidents invoked God in speeches. National days of prayer and thanksgiving were declared.[60] The Bible was quoted in Congress.

But this civil religion was broad and generic. It pointed to Providence, morality, and divine blessing, but it did not specify denominational doctrine. It provided a spiritual glue without demanding doctrinal conformity. It was the government equivalent of modern day nondenominational churches, broad enough for unity, shallow enough for comfort. It comforted the conscience but rarely challenged it.

This allowed Christianity to remain influential while still respecting pluralism, a delicate balance that would be tested over and over again.

Even as Christianity thrived, some warned of dangers. Jefferson wrote of a "wall of separation between church and state[61]," fearing that tying them together would corrupt both. The tension was set: protect the Church from the State, or the State from the Church. Baptists, often

---

[59] Robert N. Bellah, "Civil Religion in America," *Daedalus* 96, no. 1 (1967): 1–21.

[60] Abraham Lincoln, "Proclamation of Thanksgiving," October 3, 1863, in *Collected Works of Abraham Lincoln*, ed. Roy P. Basler, vol. 6 (New Brunswick, NJ: Rutgers University Press, 1953), 497–498

[61] Thomas Jefferson to the Danbury Baptists, January 1, 1802, in *The Writings of Thomas Jefferson*, vol. 16 (Washington, DC: Thomas Jefferson Memorial Association, 1903), 281–282.

persecuted in colonial days, agreed, religion needed freedom from government interference to flourish.[62]

Others feared the opposite: that without a strong Christian foundation, liberty would decay into license. They argued that the Republic's survival depended on Christian morality.

Both instincts, guarding *The River of Life* from political capture and guarding The Current of America with moral ballast, shaped our DNA.

So was America a Christian nation in its early years? In one sense, no: the government deliberately avoided an official religion. In another sense, yes: Christianity so saturated culture that it became the moral backdrop of public life. We were a nation baptized in belief but born of debate.

This paradox shaped America's identity: a secular Constitution, a religious people. A government without a church, a society steeped in church life.

For Christians today, this history offers a challenge. The early Republic reminds us that Christianity does not need political power to thrive; it flourishes when lived out freely, authentically, and with moral conviction. But it also warns us that when faith becomes too tied to national identity, it risks being watered down into civil religion rather than true discipleship, and that's a slow spiritual death.

The Church thrives when it's free, falters when it's favored, and forgets who it is when it seeks power.

Every blessing carries a warning: the moment faith becomes too cozy with power, it forgets the Cross. Every generation has to decide what

---

62 William L. Sheils, ed., *The Churches, Ireland and the Irish* (Oxford: Oxford University Press, 1989), 212–213; John Leland, "The Rights of Conscience Inalienable" (1791)

kind of Christianity it will practice, convenient or costly. The early republic chose influence. But revival always begins with repentance.

The story of America's faith is not just a record of triumphs and failures. It's a mirror. And if we look closely, we'll see that the same temptation runs through our age: to trade power for purity, applause for obedience, and influence for intimacy with God.

The question that shaped the early republic still shapes us now: Will we use our freedom to build our own kingdom, or to reveal His?[63]

🕮 Reflection Questions

1. How does the separation of church and state actually protect the church's witness?
2. Do you think America's Founders were right to see morality as essential for liberty? Why or why not?
3. In what ways can Christianity today be a moral engine for justice, as it was for abolition and reform in the early Republic?

[63] *The Holy Bible*, NIV, Matthew 6:33 and Philippians 2:10–11

Chapter Five

THE RISE OF AMERICAN CONSERVATISM

Every river eventually meets resistance. As the Current of American faith flowed through the nineteenth and early twentieth centuries, it began to change course, not because The River of Life was drying up, but because we sometimes tried to steer what was meant to flow freely.

In AP Civics class in high school, I had teacher named Mr. Scalise. At that point in his career, he was a super young teacher that everyone loved. He always started class with a debate on a certain topic and gave high schoolers the opportunity to think critically about some form of government. It was in this class that I first gained a level of interest in politics and how politics shape the way we think. Even then, I began to realize that politics shapes more than policy; it shapes how we see each other, our hopes, fears, and sense of belonging, within The Current of Culture.

He once gave us a political spectrum survey, a quiz that revealed whether we leaned conservative, liberal, or somewhere in between. It even suggested a political party that "fit" us. That was the first time, really, that I had ever put any thought into the word conservative, or liberal.

Today, when many people hear the word 'conservatism,' it often brings to mind political parties or media personalities. But in the early American Republic, conservatism meant something simpler: an instinct within *The Current* of America to preserve order, tradition, and stability.[64]

While modern readers may attach the word to one side of today's political spectrum, its early expressions were far more philosophical than partisan:

Political conservatism – caution against too much democracy, caution toward rapid change, and respect for enduring institutions.

Cultural conservatism – preserving moral order, often drawing from Christian language and practice, family life, and social hierarchies.

Both instincts would shape the nation in profound and sometimes competing ways.

Many of the same leaders who began a revolution spent their later years trying to preserve its order and balance.

John Adams often expressed concern about unchecked populism, warning that passion without principle can threaten stability.[65]

In a letter, Adams wrote: "Mobs are Sources of all kinds of Evils, Vices, and Crimes They give Rise to Treason."

In another letter he cautioned: "It is in vain to Say that Democracy is less vain[66], less proud, less selfish, less ambitious or less avaricious than

---

[64] Russell Kirk, *The Conservative Mind: From Burke to Eliot*, 7th ed. (Chicago: Regnery Books, 1986), 7–9.

[65] John Adams to James Sullivan, May 26, 1776, in *The Works of John Adams*, ed. Charles Francis Adams, vol. 9 (Boston: Little, Brown and Company, 1854), 375–376.

[66] John Adams, *The Letters of John and Abigail Adams*, ed. Frank Shuffelton (New York: Penguin Classics, 2004), 214–215.

Aristocracy or Monarchy when unchecked, [passions] produce the same Effects of Fraud, Violence and Cruelty."

And more broadly, he observed: "Democracy is more bloody than either [aristocracy or monarchy] Remember, democracy never lasts long. It soon wastes, exhausts, and murders itself."[67]

These quotes show his deep worries about unchecked popular rule devolving into instability or oppression.

Alexander Hamilton (my name is Alexander Hammmilllton) pushed for a strong central government, fearing the instability of too much local control.[68]

Hamilton argued for executive strength: "Energy in the executive is a leading character in the definition of good government. It is essential to the steady administration of the laws to the security of liberty against the enterprises of faction and of anarchy."

He also warned of the danger of local or minority obstruction: "Men of factious tempers, of local prejudices, or of sinister designs, may, by intrigue, by corruption first obtain the suffrages, and then betray the interests of the people." [69]

In Federalist No. 23, he emphasized that the federal government must have sufficient vigor to preserve order and unity: (Paraphrase) The federal government must be able to meet national defense, internal security, and other essential functions, which weak governments cannot do. These show Hamilton's conviction that too much deference

---

[67] John Adams to John Taylor, December 17, 1814, in *The Works of John Adams*, vol. 6 (Boston: Little, Brown and Company, 1851), 484.

[68] Alexander Hamilton, *The Federalist No. 70*, in *The Federalist Papers*, ed. Clinton Rossiter (New York: Signet Classics, 2003), 423–424.

[69] Alexander Hamilton, *The Federalist No. 10*, in *The Federalist Papers*, ed. Clinton Rossiter (New York: Signet Classics, 2003), 77–79.

to local or state authority risked fragmentation, gridlock, or domination by particular interests.

Each of them sensed that freedom without virtue could eventually consume itself.

George Washington in his Farewell Address urged Americans to avoid political factions and maintain moral order.[70]

Washington warned: "Let me now take a more comprehensive view, and warn you in the most solemn manner against the baneful effects of the spirit of party, generally. The alternate domination of one faction over another, sharpened by the spirit of revenge is itself a frightful despotism."

He also expressed concern that parties would be used by unscrupulous men: "However [political parties] may now and then answer popular ends, they are likely to become potent engines, by which cunning, ambitious, and unprincipled men will be enabled to subvert the power of the people destroying afterward the very engines which have lifted them to unjust dominion."

And he cautioned about their more routine mischiefs: "The common and continual mischiefs of the spirit of party distract the public councils and enfeeble the public administration. It agitates the community with ill-founded jealousies and false alarms, kindles animosity foments occasionally riot and insurrection opens the door to foreign influence and corruption "Washington urged citizens to resist the seductive appeal of faction and to protect the moral fabric and unity of the republic. Even Washington recognized how the same soil that grew freedom could also grow division.

---

[70] George Washington, *Farewell Address*, September 19, 1796, in *The Writings of George Washington*, ed. John C. Fitzpatrick, vol. 35 (Washington, DC: US Government Printing Office, 1940), 226–229.

To these leaders, conservatism was about preserving the fragile republic they had created, making sure liberty did not spiral into chaos. At its best, it sought to steady *The Current* of America with moral ballast drawn from the nation's Christian vocabulary. At its worst, it risked mistaking cultural stability for Kingdom faithfulness.

I believe that Christianity became the glue that helped stabilize the young nation. Churches doubled as schoolhouses and Sunday sermons discussed civic virtue.

In this sense, Christianity *was* functioning conservatively: it preserved order, reinforced moral norms, and reminded citizens of accountability to God. Faith steadied freedom, but it sometimes risked confusing faithfulness with familiarity.

But the greatest moral test of early American conservatism was slavery. For many in the South, 'conservatism' came to mean defending the existing social order, including, tragically, the institution of slavery. Christian rhetoric was tragically used to justify slavery, with pastors quoting Scripture to defend hierarchy and obedience.[71]

At the same time, Christian abolitionists, from William Lloyd Garrison to the Quakers, insisted that true conservatism should conserve justice and human dignity, not injustice.[72] They pointed to the biblical truth that all people are made in God's image.

This divide reveals the tension within conservatism: when preserving tradition becomes the highest good, even harmful traditions can be unintentionally protected. The Current of Culture can carry sin forward under the name of "order."

---

[71] Mark A. Noll, *The Civil War as a Theological Crisis* (Chapel Hill: University of North Carolina Press, 2006), 32–36.

[72] William Lloyd Garrison, *The Liberator* (January 1, 1831), 1; Larry Ceplair, *The Public Years of Sarah and Angelina Grimké* (New York: Columbia University Press, 1989), 21–23.

There is a hilarious episode of Parks and Recreation where the town of Pawnee celebrates "Ted Day" every year because the word "tea" in their town charter looked like "ted." While clearly a handwriting discrepancy, the town insisted on celebrating "Ted Day" by throwing a person named Ted into a body of water, instead of the obvious choice of overtaxed tea, like the Boston Tea Party. You can imagine how frustrated the "Teds" of Pawnee had become with this tradition. The whole episode hinges on the idea that some traditions aren't worth conserving. Kingdom conservatism preserves what is holy; cultural conservatism can sometimes cling to what is merely habitual.

After the Civil War (1861–1865), conservatism took on new meanings[73]:

Politically, it often meant resisting rapid social change, especially regarding reconstruction and civil rights for freed slaves. Economically, it began to emphasize property rights, free markets, and limited government intervention. Culturally, it leaned on Christianity to preserve family structures, morality, and community stability.

A few years ago, I was the director of cinematography on a Christmas movie in a town called New Richmond, Ohio. This was near Cincinnati, Ohio and it was the home of an old church from this era called the Cranston Memorial Presbyterian Church. This church played an important role in the Underground Railroad and even had speakers like John Rankin, James Birney, George Beecher (Harriet Beecher Stowe's brother), and Calvin Stowe (Harriet Beecher Stowe's husband.) When I shot there, I could feel the history all around me, knowing that this church was an epicenter of freedom, and a beacon of hope for many slaves who were escaping the South. A holy kind of weight still

---

[73] Eric Foner, Reconstruction: America's Unfinished Revolution, 1863–1877 (New York: Harper & Row, 1988), 184–188.

lingers there that is a memory of churches that chose The River of Life over the dominant current of their time.[74]

Unfortunately, in the late 1800s, not all churches were like the Cranston Memorial Presbyterian Church. After the Civil War, while many churches shifted away from overt defenses of slavery, there were still some congregations and leaders who continued to champion pro-slavery or pro"–Lost Cause" theology. A well-documented example comes from the Southern Presbyterian Church (Presbyterian Church in the United States) in the 1860s and 1870s. For every church that worked to free slaves, another tragically found ways to justify bondage through theology rather than chains.

One striking case is Robert Lewis Dabney, a Southern Presbyterian theologian, Confederate chaplain, and postwar church leader. Even after emancipation, Dabney insisted that slavery was biblically sanctioned and that Reconstruction was a moral and theological disaster.[75] In his "Defense of Virginia, and Through Her, of the South" (1867), written in the immediate post–Civil War period, he argued that slavery was "the righteous, God-ordained relation of master and servant," and that abolition was an assault on divine order. Dabney preached and published works reinforcing this worldview, influencing generations of Southern churchmen.

Even theology can become restrictive when carried by *The Current of Culture* rather than nourished by *The River of Life.*

Similarly, Southern Baptist Convention leaders after the war doubled down on a pro-slavery theology, framing the Confederacy as a

---

[74] *Cranston Memorial Presbyterian Church Historical Society*, "Underground Railroad Heritage in New Richmond, Ohio," accessed October 15, 2025, https://cranstonpresbyterian.org/history.

[75] Robert Lewis Dabney, Defense of Virginia, and Through Her, of the South (New York: E. J. Hale & Son, 1867), 52–54.

Christian cause.[76] Even after slavery ended, some churches preached that hierarchy was holy. They read Scripture not to be transformed, transformed, but to be justified. Some churches even publicly read resolutions declaring slavery "in full accordance with the Holy Scriptures" and lamented its end as a judgment on the South. Some pulpits read the Bible downstream, letting the current decide the meaning, rather than reading it at the Source.

So, Christianity once again played a double role: inspiring movements for justice while also being invoked to defend segregation and hierarchy in the South.

By the late 1800s, American conservatism had a recognizable shape[77]:

- Suspicion of radical change – whether abolitionists, women's suffrage, or labor unions.
- Emphasis on moral order – Christianity was expected to keep society morally sound.
- Defense of economic freedom – businesses and property rights were to be protected from government interference.

It was a worldview built to steady the ship, but at times, that steadiness slowed the tide of justice.

Yet conservatism was not monolithic. Some sought to conserve comfort; others fought to conserve conscience.

As the 19th century closed, Christianity and conservatism were closely linked in the public imagination:

---

[76] *Proceedings of the Southern Baptist Convention*, 1863 (Richmond, VA: H. K. Ellyson, 1863), 27–28; Curtis W. Freeman, *Baptist Roots* (Valley Forge: Judson Press, 1999), 101–103.

[77] Patrick Allitt, The Conservatives: Ideas and Personalities Throughout American History (New Haven: Yale University Press, 2009), 45–47.

- Politicians invoked God in speeches.[78]
- Churches reinforced patriotism through hymns, prayers, and civic events.
- Family values and Christian morality were seen as essential for national strength.

This blending was not yet the partisan alliance we see today, but the seeds were planted: conservatism borrowed moral authority from the Church, and the Church borrowed cultural protection from conservatism. Each leaned on the other for legitimacy, Christianity offered moral weight, conservatism offered cultural stability.[79]

But this legacy was mixed: conservatism preserved both noble ideals (like liberty and order) and sinful injustices (like slavery and segregation). Christianity too was divided, sometimes prophetic, calling the nation higher; other times complicit, blessing the status quo.

Whenever the Church flowed with *The River of Life*, it confronted sin, even cherished, cultural sin. Whenever it drifted with The Current of America, it sometimes blessed what it should have buried.

The question this leaves us with still echoes today: When Christians align with conservatism, are we conserving the values of the Kingdom, or merely the comforts of our culture?

Jesus didn't call us to comfortable.

He called us to die daily, pick up a cross, and follow him.

The River of Life doesn't depend on who controls the current; it depends on who abides in the Source.

---

[78] Abraham Lincoln, "Second Inaugural Address," March 4, 1865, in *Collected Works of Abraham Lincoln*, ed. Roy P. Basler, vol. 8 (New Brunswick, NJ: Rutgers University Press, 1953), 332–333.

[79] George M. Marsden, Fundamentalism and American Culture: The Shaping of Twentieth-Century Evangelicalism 1870–1925, 2nd ed. (New York: Oxford University Press, 2006), 5–7.

The Kingdom does not ride The Current of America; it redirects it, toward repentance, justice, and love.[80]

🕮 Reflection Questions

1. When does conserving tradition help preserve what is good, and when does it risk protecting what is sinful?
2. How should Christians today discern between conserving biblical truth and conserving cultural comfort?
3. In what ways can conservatism be a blessing to society, and in what ways can it become an idol?

80 *The Holy Bible*, New International Version (Colorado Springs: Biblica, 2011), Luke 9:23; John 7:38.

Chapter Six

MODERN FAITH IN AN INDUSTRIAL WORLD

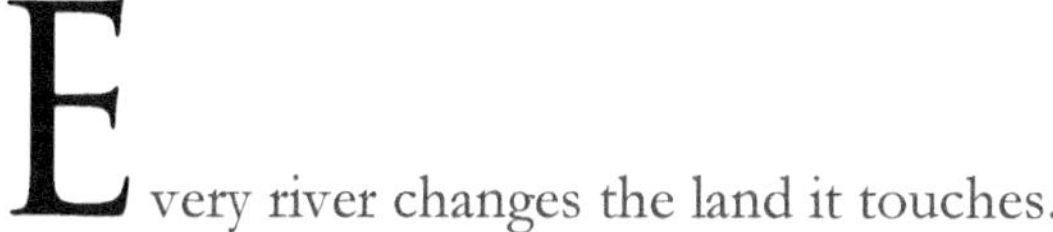

Every river changes the land it touches.

After the Civil War, *The Current* of America of faith entered new terrain, the floodplain of modernity.

The waters that once ran through revival tents and open fields now flowed between smokestacks and city streets.

The same current that once carried pilgrims across oceans was now forced through pipes and power lines.

And somewhere in that mechanical hum, the still, small voice of God seemed harder to hear amid the sound of progress.

The nation was moving faster than ever before. Steam replaced soil. The factory replaced the farm. And the Church, caught between its past and its future, tried to decide whether to flow with The Current of Culture or stand still in *The River of Life*.

As the Industrial Revolution transformed America, the Church faced a question it had never encountered:

What does it mean to follow Jesus in a world built by machines?

Faith that once spoke to farmers now had to speak to factory workers. The language of the plow had to learn the dialect of the assembly line.

The gospel had to find its footing on crowded sidewalks and its echo in neighborhoods darkened by smog.

Out of that tension came the Social Gospel, a movement that believed the message of Christ must heal both souls and systems.

Preachers like Walter Rauschenbusch and reformers like Jane Addams saw sin not only in the heart but in the housing crisis, the sweatshop, and the hunger line.

They asked, "If the Kingdom of God truly came to earth, would it look like this?"

They fed the poor, fought for justice, and believed *The River of Life*'s mercy could flood the world's broken banks.

But not everyone agreed on what that flood should wash away.

As the Social Gospel rose, Fundamentalism emerged in response.

Where reformers saw faith as movement, fundamentalists saw it as foundation. They believed the rising tide of science and modernism was eroding the bedrock of belief. So they built boundaries. They reinforced doctrine. They anchored their hope in the immovable Word of God.

Both sides claimed to protect the river, one wanted to let it flow freely through the city; the other to keep it pure upstream.

Both loved truth. Both feared compromise. And both, in their own way, forgot that rivers are meant to move. When faith stops moving, it stagnates. When faith turns inward and seeks control, moral, intellectual, or political, the living water grows still.

The battle lines of modern Christianity weren't just drawn in pulpits, they were drawn in hearts.

In 1925, the entire nation gathered around one courtroom in Dayton, Tennessee. It was July, hot, humid, and heavy. Inside, a high school teacher named John Scopes stood trial for teaching evolution. Outside, vendors sold Bible verses and cold lemonade side by side. It felt like a fair and a funeral at once. The Scopes "Monkey" Trial became more than a legal debate; it became a spectacle, a sermon performed for the modern world.

Prosecutor William Jennings Bryan defended Scripture. Defense attorney Clarence Darrow defended reason. And the radio, a new, unseen river of its own, carried their voices across the nation.

When the dust settled, faith had technically "won" the case, but lost the narrative. Modern America began to see Christianity as fearful and outdated. The Church, once the shaper of culture, began to be treated as its punchline.

But deep beneath the noise, something was shifting. The current hadn't dried up, it had gone underground, waiting for spring.

Then came 1929. The market crashed, factories closed, and dreams evaporated overnight.[81] Men who built fortunes stood in breadlines. Mothers prayed over empty tables. For the first time in a generation, America discovered the limits of progress. When the towers of wealth fell, the wells of prayer reopened. And in that crisis, *The River of Life* rose again.

Revivals swept across the country. Tent meetings filled. Preachers like Aimee Semple McPherson dramatized the gospel on radio waves, while

---

[81] David M. Kennedy, Freedom from Fear: The American People in Depression and War, 1929–1945 (New York: Oxford University Press, 1999), 32–34.

Billy Sunday shouted it from stadium pulpits. Despair drove people back to the river.

They brought energy, urgency, and the kind of hope that could pierce despair. But this revival looked different. It was louder, faster, more spectacular, like the world it preached to.

The Church had learned the rhythms of the machine. Faith had learned efficiency, but risked forgetting intimacy.

Faith had become efficient. And while the gospel was still true, its delivery began to feel more like production than participation.

The industrial revolution didn't just change how we worked. It changed how we worshiped. Before, church life was organic; people lived near one another, shared meals, bore burdens. But modernity trained us to think in systems, schedules, and outputs. So when faith adapted to the industrial age, it often adopted its methods. The sacred had been scheduled.

We began to structure churches like factories: predictable inputs... and a process of spiritual formation that risked making every believer look the same. Heaven doesn't mass-produce holiness.

It worked, for a while.

The "machine church" produced converts, campaigns, and capital. But in the process, we risked losing the mystery. When discipleship becomes mechanical, it's easy to lose sensitivity to the Spirit's flow. We start mistaking numbers for depth, activity for obedience. We mistake growth for godliness, and movement for maturity. *The River of Life*'s presence cannot be automated. It refuses to run through pipes of predictability. It moves as it wills, carving canyons, flooding plains, and sometimes overturning the structures we build along its edge. Industrial Christianity gave us efficiency, but the Spirit calls us back to intimacy. It invites us off the assembly line and into the water.

By the 1930s, radios hummed in nearly every home. For the first time, people could hear the gospel without ever stepping into a church. Faith had found a new medium, and a new temptation. The good news was accessible to millions. The bad news was that it became marketable to millions.

Charisma often began to overshadow character. Production sometimes replaced presence. And soon, churches found themselves competing not for souls, but for airtime. Still, God used even this.

During World War II, soldiers carried pocket-sized Bibles into battle. Chaplains preached from foxholes.[82] In the silence between shellfire, the words of Jesus still cut through: "Peace I leave with you; my peace I give you."

When the world went mad, *The River of Life* still flowed.

When the war ended in 1945, the nation exhaled, and then inhaled ambition again. Factories returned to making cars instead of weapons. Suburbs sprawled. Baby cries filled the air.[83] And beneath it all, the hum of industry began to echo inside the sanctuary.

But by the 1960s, the hum of industry was drowned out by helicopters. The same nation that had rebuilt the world after World War II now watched its sons fly into another kind of fire.[84] For a generation raised on postwar confidence, the Vietnam War became a mirror, reflecting not strength, but strain. Progress had promised peace; instead, the machine produced body bags.

For the first time, the assembly line of American optimism jammed. Television screens, our new stained-glass windows, flickered with

---

[82] Jonathan Ebel, Faith in the Fight: Religion and the American Soldier in the Great War (Princeton, NJ: Princeton University Press, 2010), 143–145.

[83] Lizabeth Cohen, A Consumers 'Republic: The Politics of Mass Consumption in Postwar America (New York: Vintage, 2003), 112–115.

[84] Religion News Service, "The Vietnam Years: How the Conflict Ripped the Nation's Religious Fabric," September 8, 2017.

nightly images of napalm, protest, and funerals.[85] What had once been distant became intimate. The war came into the living room, and with it, a creeping realization: the nation that claimed to be "under God" was losing its sense of God altogether.

In the factories and the pews alike, people began to ask different questions. Not "How do we build more?" but "Why are we building this at all?" The sons of churchgoing families marched in protest rather than in parades.[86] The youth who had grown up pledging allegiance to both God and country began to question whether those two allegiances could coexist.

For many, the Vietnam era was the death of innocence, and the birth of cynicism. Faith, once seen as an anchor of certainty, started to look like another arm of the establishment. Some pastors preached patriotism; others preached peace. [87] Sanctuaries became divided between those who prayed for victory and those who prayed for withdrawal. [88] And in the tension between pulpit and protest, a generation lost trust in institutions, political and religious.

The Church had long been comfortable in the rhythm of predictability: Sunday suits, hymns of triumph, tidy sermons about a God of order. But now, that order felt complicit in chaos. Many young people concluded that the Church's polished language couldn't speak to the pain of a world on fire.[89] So they left the sanctuary and searched for the Spirit elsewhere.

---

[85] Religion News Service, "The Vietnam Years," September 8, 2017.

[86] David Mislin, "How Vietnam War Protests Accelerated the Rise of the Christian Right," *Smithsonian Magazine*, May 3, 2018.

[87] Sean McFarland, "How American Christians Responded to the Vietnam War" (Taylor University, 2023), 12–15.

[88] Faith and War: How Christians Debated the Cold and Vietnam Wars (New York: NYU Press, 2016), ch. 2.

[89] George Bogaski, "American Protestants and the Debate over the Vietnam War," *Christian Century*, October 29, 2014.

Yet even as denominations split and pews emptied, something unexpected was happening on the streets and beaches. While one current of the culture raged with war and revolution, another began to ripple with renewal. [90] The Jesus Movement, born from the counterculture, became a kind of spiritual protest of its own. Hippies with guitars gathered under the open sky, preaching peace through a Person, not a policy. They had rejected the machine of American Christianity but rediscovered the man from Galilee.[91]

Once again, *The River of Life* found a new channel. It flowed through barefoot believers, coffeehouse Bible studies, and baptisms in the Pacific. It ran through movements that valued presence over production, simplicity over systems, encounter over efficiency. They didn't need a steeple; they needed the Spirit. And in the unlikeliest places, revival returned, not to the institutions that had industrialized faith, but to the margins that still believed it could be real.

The Vietnam War didn't just divide a country; it dismantled illusions.[92] It showed that progress cannot sanctify, that power cannot redeem, and that control cannot create peace.[93] In its aftermath, America's soul stood in ruins, and in that rubble, the River began to flow again. For when the machinery of certainty breaks down, people begin to thirst for something living once more. America was ready to build. But the Church was ready to brand. We began to model churches after

---

[90] Jennifer Esch, "How Christian Political Factions Influenced America During the Vietnam War," *Michigan Journal of History* (2014).

[91] Faith and War, ch. 5.

[92] The Gospel Coalition, "Ken Burns '*The Vietnam War* Is Worth Your Time," September 25, 2017.

[93]" The Biblical Basis For and Against the Vietnam War," *Times of Israel Blogs*, June 15, 2025.

corporations, measure ministry by productivity, and package sermons like products.[94] We called it excellence.

But sometimes it hid a desire for control more than a devotion to calling. The irony is haunting:

- We industrialized the very gospel that once turned the world upside down.

- We built systems so strong that it became easy to forget how to depend on the Spirit.

And yet, even then, *The River of Life* kept running. Because the river is never still. It runs beneath every building, every empire, and every generation's noise. It flows from the throne of God, not the boardroom of man. And when the dams of our pride break, it always finds its way forward.

The River of Life moves at the pace of people, not productivity.[95] It pauses for the one lost sheep. It stops for the bleeding woman. It sits at the well at noon, waiting for a single thirsty heart. You can't automate that. That's not inefficiency, it's incarnation.

The twentieth century taught us many things, but perhaps none more sobering than this: Progress cannot redeem us. We can harness power and build nations, but we cannot manufacture holiness.[96]

As the factories quieted and the fear of another war began to rise, America turned once again to religion, not out of devotion, but defense. And thus, a new kind of faith was born: one baptized in

[94] Rick Warren, The Purpose Driven Church: Growth Without Compromising Your Message and Mission (Grand Rapids: Zondervan, 1995), 29–31; David F. Wells, No Place for Truth: Or Whatever Happened to Evangelical Theology? (Grand Rapids: Eerdmans, 1993), 56–59.

[95] Luke 15:4–7; Mark 5:25–34; John 4:5–26 (New International Version)

[96] Jacques Ellul, *The Technological Society*, trans. John Wilkinson (New York: Vintage, 1964), 235–238.

patriotism, stirred by fear, and clothed in red, white, and blue. For many, patriotism began to feel like piety.

That story, the story of Cold War Religion, is the next bend in the river. But before we turn the page, we must remember: *The Current of Culture* will always pull us toward control, but *The River of Life* calls us into surrender.[97] One builds with steel and strategy. The other flows with Spirit and sacrifice.

And in every generation, we must decide which current we'll follow.

The early industrialists mastered the art of motion; the early disciples mastered the art of stillness. And one of those changed the world forever.

We can't compete with the world's efficiency, but we were never meant to. Our strength isn't in production. It's in presence. And if we will slow down long enough to listen, we might hear the faint hum of another rhythm, the unhurried current of the Spirit, still flowing, still calling, still alive beneath all our machinery.

Because revival doesn't begin when the machine runs faster. It begins when we shut it down.[98]

---

[97] Philippians 2:5–11 (NIV)
[98] Psalm 46:10 (NIV)

Chapter Seven

COLD WAR RELIGION

Growing up in West Virginia, "October Sky" was a big deal. For some reason, it's one of those memories that stuck.

In 1957, the coal-mining town of Coalwood, West Virginia is shaken when the Soviet Union launches Sputnik into orbit[99]. For the United States, it's more than just a satellite; it's a symbol of Soviet power in the escalating Cold War. For young Homer Hickam, watching that speck of light move across the night sky ignites a dream: if the Russians can reach space, maybe he can too. For Homer, the stars were calling; for America, they felt like a warning.

Together with his friends Roy Lee, O'Dell, and Quentin, Homer forms the "Rocket Boys." Their experiments begin as small-town curiosities but soon draw national attention. What starts as a hobby becomes part of a bigger story, the competition between nations for scientific dominance. Homer's teacher, Miss Riley, reminds him that America needs minds like his if it hopes to compete with the Soviets.

---

99 Homer H. Hickam Jr., *Rocket Boys: A Memoir* (New York: Delacorte Press, 1998), 3–7.

Yet, this ambition clashes with the world closer to home. Homer's father, John, is the mine superintendent, and he views rockets as a childish distraction from Coalwood's reality: coal is the lifeblood of the town, and the mine is where every boy belongs. Their father-son conflict mirrors the broader divide between tradition and progress, between a community fixed underground and a generation that dares to look to the skies. A similar tension stirred in the nation's soul: would we be led more by fear or by faith, by *The Current* of America's anxiety or by *The River of Life*'s calling?

As the Rocket Boys 'designs improve, their rockets soar higher, symbols of youthful determination in a Cold War world where scientific achievement is tied to national survival. When Homer wins first place at the National Science Fair, his triumph isn't just personal; it's a small-town boy's contribution to America's race against the Soviets.

This film was my introduction to the Cold War. I remember watching it on a charter bus, on a VHS Tape (yep), heading to a Cincinnati Reds Baseball Game with my Dad's work. That's when I first sensed that fear could be as powerful a fuel as faith, a rival current running beneath the surface.

Like Homer Hickam's rockets breaking free from the pull of gravity, faith in mid-century America was struggling to rise above the weight of fear. In our pursuit of wrestling with Christianity and America, the Cold War was a defining challenge in the mid-20th century.

The Soviet Union loomed as both a military threat and an ideological enemy. At stake was not just territory or weapons, but worldviews: atheistic communism versus religious democracy.[100] Sermons warned that Moscow stood where Babylon once stood. Both worldviews were

---

[100] John Lewis Gaddis, *The Cold War: A New History* (New York: Penguin Press, 2005), 34–38.

eschatological in their own way, Marxism promised a secular heaven; Christianity, a divine one.

For many Americans, this was not just a political conflict, it was a spiritual battle. Communism denied God, denied individual rights, and exalted the state.[101] In contrast, America portrayed itself as the land of liberty, faith, and free enterprise. *The Current* of America told a story about itself; *The River of Life* told a different one. The Cold War wasn't fought only with missiles, but also with powerful national stories.

This context helped form a new blend of conservatism and Christianity, one that would shape the nation for generations.

During the Cold War, American leaders leaned heavily on religious language to distinguish the United States from the Soviet Union.

- In 1954, the words "under God" were added to the Pledge of Allegiance.[102]
- In 1956, "In God We Trust" became the official national motto.[103]

Presidents regularly invoked divine blessing in speeches, portraying America as a nation guided by Providence.[104]

This was not the Christianity of revival tents or denominational creeds. It was civil religion, a broad, patriotic spirituality that united citizens against a godless enemy. It united many, but not always around the deeper the truths of *The River of Life.*

---

[101] Karl Marx, *Critique of Hegel s Philosophy of Right* (Cambridge: Cambridge University Press, 1970), 64–65.

[102] U.S. Congress, Public Law 83-396, July 14, 1954; House of Representatives Congressional Record, 100th Cong., 2nd sess., 1954, 8618.

[103] U.S. Congress, Public Law 84-140, July 30, 1956; National Archives and Records Administration, Records of the U.S. House of Representatives.

[104] Dwight D. Eisenhower, "Inaugural Address," January 20, 1953, *Public Papers of the Presidents of the United States* (Washington, DC: GPO, 1953), 1–3.

Growing up, I thought "under God" and "In God We Trust" would have been staples of our nation from the time of the founding fathers. Based on the rhetoric of being a Christian nation, that would have made sense. However, those two phrases are less than 100 years old in terms of being in any official capacity with the United States. It doesn't make the statements any less important, but it is a reminder of how recent some cherished symbols are, even when they feel as though they've always been there. These new slogans became tributaries to *The Current* of America, spiritual in sound, sometimes thin in theological roots.

Church attendance surged in the 1950s. Billy Graham filled stadiums with crusades that blended gospel preaching with patriotic fervor.[105] Politicians sought his blessing. Families saw churchgoing as both a spiritual duty and a civic expectation. The crowd could comfort us; the cross would confront us. Too often, comfort won our attention.

Conservatism found in Christianity the perfect moral partner:

- Christianity upheld the family as the bedrock of society.
- It promoted personal virtue, discipline, and hard work, values that aligned with free-market ideals.
- It provided a moral contrast to communism's atheism and collectivism.[106]

For many, being a "good American" meant being a "churchgoing Christian." It was a marriage of morality and might, faith sanctified, freedom glorified. The Current of America borrowed the language of *The River of Life*.

105 William Martin, A Prophet with Honor: The Billy Graham Story (New York: William Morrow, 1991), 214–219.

106 Kevin M. Kruse, One Nation Under God: How Corporate America Invented Christian America (New York: Basic Books, 2015), 52–56.

But there was also anxiety. The Supreme Court, in cases like Engel v. Vitale (1962), ruled against state-sponsored school prayer.[107] Later rulings limited Bible readings in classrooms. To many Christians, this felt like a retreat from the nation's heritage, or a direct attack against Christians themselves.

This *perception* of persecution has resurfaced often in our public life. Each election of my lifetime makes "prayer in school" feel like something that was taken away in recent years. However, Engel v. Vitale happened in 1962, specifically to defend the first amendment of the constitution. Misunderstood claims of persecution often repeat through history. They are dangerous because they are like the story of the little boy who cried wolf. At some point, when real persecution comes (as Jesus predicted it would), will our witness be taken seriously? Perhaps the deeper question was never whether prayer was removed from schools, but whether it remained in the hearts of believers, where *The River of Life* actually flows.

Conservatives began to warn that America was drifting from God.[108] The removal of prayer from schools, the rise of secular education, and cultural shifts in the 1960s and 70s fueled the sense that the moral fabric was unraveling.

This fear would become the seedbed for a new political movement. A new version of civil religion began to crystallize, a sanctified nationalism carried along by *The Current of Culture.*

While civil religion united Americans, it carried dangers:

- It often blurred the line between true discipleship and cultural Christianity.

[107] *Engel v. Vitale*, 370 U.S. 421 (1962).
[108] Daniel K. Williams, God's Own Party: The Making of the Christian Right (New York: Oxford University Press, 2010), 12–14.

  - Being "American" was often equated with being "Christian," regardless of personal faith. Church membership was seen as a civic duty rather than a commitment to Christ.
  - Even Billy Graham warned against "easy-believism" where patriotism and faith blurred.

- It made faith a marker of patriotism rather than a call to personal transformation.

  - The addition of "under God" to the Pledge of Allegiance (1954) and "In God We Trust" as the national motto (1956) tied Christianity to nationalism. By the 1970s–80s, questioning these symbols sometimes was received as un-American rather than a matter of religious conscience.

- It sometimes reduced Christianity to slogans and rituals, eclipsing the call of the gospel.

  - Political rallies often used Bible verses or Christian hymns as rallying cries without theological context (e.g., "If my people will humble themselves" from 2 Chronicles 7:14 was used widely in political campaigns).
  - Campaigns often invoked "God and country" in slogans, sometimes more as cultural shorthand than calls to genuine repentance or gospel transformation.

Still, for millions of Americans, civil religion provided stability in a time of global tension. It reassured them that God was on America's side.

We need to pause here. "God being on America's side" is something that has been woven into the fabric of our nation since the beginning. This assumption has shaped every war, every election, and every sermon that ever draped a flag behind a pulpit.

From the very beginning, American colonists often interpreted their story through a biblical lens. Puritan settlers in New England believed they were a "city upon a hill"[109] (John Winthrop, 1630), chosen by God to model righteousness to the world. This sense of divine mission gave birth to what historians call American exceptionalism.

As we mentioned before, during the Revolutionary War, ministers preached "political sermons" that cast the fight for independence as a holy cause. They compared Britain to Pharaoh and America to Israel being delivered by God's hand. When the colonies prevailed against the greatest empire in the world, many Americans took it as confirmation that God had blessed their cause.

In the 1860s, both North and South claimed God's favor. Union soldiers sang The Battle Hymn of the Republic ("His truth is marching on"), while Confederates saw themselves as a Christian nation defending biblical order. Abraham Lincoln wisely noted the irony: "Both read the same Bible and pray to the same God, and each invokes His aid against the other."[110] Lincoln's humility reminds us: *The River of Life*'s justice never belongs to one bank.

In the 20th century, this conviction deepened. In World War I, Woodrow Wilson framed the US as making "the world safe for democracy," with religious undertones.[111] In World War II, slogans like "God Bless America" (popularized by Irving Berlin's song in 1938, then widely sung during the war) reinforced the idea that America's

---

109 John Winthrop, "A Model of Christian Charity" (1630), in *Collections of the Massachusetts Historical Society*, 3rd ser., vol. 7 (Boston: Massachusetts Historical Society, 1838), 31–48.

110 Abraham Lincoln, *Second Inaugural Address*, March 4, 1865, in *Collected Works of Abraham Lincoln*, ed. Roy P. Basler, vol. 8 (New Brunswick, NJ: Rutgers University Press, 1953), 333.

111 Woodrow Wilson, "Address to Congress Requesting a Declaration of War Against Germany," April 2, 1917, *Congressional Record*, 65th Cong., 1st sess., 1917, 224–225.

fight against fascism was righteous.[112] Soldiers carried pocket Bibles into battle, and presidents invoked God in speeches.

And then we get to the Cold War, which sharpened this belief like never before. The Soviet Union's atheistic communism was seen as the enemy of God Himself. Politicians, from Eisenhower to Reagan, framed the conflict as a cosmic struggle between good (Christian America) and evil (godless Soviet Union).[113]

All of this fed into a distinctly American civil religion, a belief that the nation itself had a divine mission. Patriotism and Christianity often blended, leading many to assume that being American meant being Christian, and that God's blessing was tied to national strength. We sometimes stopped asking whether God was with us, and began to assume He was

By the end of the Cold War era, the fusion of Christianity and conservatism looked something like this[114]:

- Conservatism provided the political framework, anti-communism, free markets, strong defense, and traditional values.
- Christianity provided the moral and spiritual legitimacy.
- This partnership was powerful, but also precarious. It made Christianity appear inseparable from a particular political ideology. The stage was set for the 1970s and 80s, when this

[112] Irving Berlin, "God Bless America," 1938; Library of Congress, Performing Arts Encyclopedia, "Historical Context of 'God Bless America, " 'accessed October 2025.

[113] Ronald Reagan, "Evil Empire Speech," March 8, 1983, *Public Papers of the Presidents of the United States* (Washington, DC: GPO, 1983), 359–364; Eisenhower, "Inaugural Address," 1953.

[114] Kevin M. Schultz, Tri-Faith America: How Catholics and Jews Held Postwar Pluralism Together (New York: Oxford University Press, 2011), 88–91.

> fusion would become formalized in movements like the Moral Majority.[115]

Faith gave politics a halo; politics gave faith a platform, and both began to shape The Current of America more than they submitted to *The River of Life*.[116]

The Cold War redefined American conservatism as not just a political philosophy, but a spiritual defense of faith and freedom against atheistic communism. Christianity became tightly bound to national identity, often symbolized by the cross and the flag standing side by side. Very similar to the stage, at the Baptist Church in West Virginia in which I grew up. American flag on one side, Christian flag on the other. The river of faith that once flowed from humble revivals channeled increasingly into political canals.

This moment in history shows both the strength and weakness of the Christian-conservative alliance. It gave the church cultural influence, but it also risked diluting the gospel into nationalism. *Influence without intimacy often drifts towards idolatry.*

The challenge that emerged then, and continues now, is this: Can Christians engage the public square without blocking the flow of The River of Grace? The Cold War taught us how easy it is to confuse the flow of the Spirit with the tide of power.

While the world braced for fallout, God was still forming faith underground, in prayer groups, in quiet revivals, in small gatherings that remembered the gospel wasn't about proving our power but surrendering to His.

---

[115] Frances FitzGerald, The Evangelicals: The Struggle to Shape America (New York: Simon & Schuster, 2017), 312–315.

[116] William Martin, With God on Our Side: The Rise of the Religious Right in America (New York: Broadway Books, 1996), 44–47.

Every generation faces its own Cold War, some external, some internal. Fear will always promise to hold us together faster than faith can. But fear can't sustain what love alone can build. Fear may rally a nation, but only love can redeem it.[117]

The Church must decide again: Will we cling to the safety of civil religion, or embrace the vulnerability of the Kingdom? Because *The River of Life* doesn't flow from missiles or monuments. It flows from mercy, still moving, still calling, even through the fallout of our fear.[118]

🕮 REFLECTION QUESTIONS

1. In what ways did the Cold War strengthen Christianity's public influence in America?
2. How did civil religion blur the line between authentic discipleship and cultural Christianity?
3. What parallels do you see today with the way faith and patriotism are blended in public life?

---

[117] 1 John 4:18 (New International Version).
[118] Micah 6:8 (NIV).

Part II

THE FUSION - WHEN FAITH AND POLITICS COLLIDED

When the current of heaven meets the current of earth, the water churns.

Here we trace the moment that mixture became muddled, when devotion to Jesus intertwined with the pursuit of national power.

These chapters reveal how the fusion of faith and politics didn't happen overnight, but drop by drop, story by story, until the two became nearly indistinguishable.

Chapter Eight

THE MORAL MAJORITY AND THE RELIGIOUS RIGHT

The choir swells. The preacher grips the pulpit. Behind him, an American flag flutters as he declares, "We must take back our country for God." The words echoed through sanctuaries across America, not as rebellion, but as a rallying cry from a Church longing to be heard again.

It's the early 1980s, and something new is stirring in America, a movement that promised to make faith matter again.

For decades, the Church had watched the culture drift. Prayer was removed from schools. Abortion was legalized. Families fractured. Pastors preached about holiness while headlines preached despair. The Church that once shaped the nation began to feel like it was losing its voice. And in the silence between Sunday sermons and Monday headlines, fear began to speak louder than faith.

Rewind 20 years.

By the late 1960s, America was in turmoil. The sexual revolution challenged traditional morality. The civil rights movement exposed deep racial injustice and shifted political alignments. The Supreme

Court legalized abortion in Roe v. Wade (1973).[119] Vietnam and Watergate eroded trust in government.

For many Christians, especially evangelicals, this felt like the unraveling of America's moral fabric. School prayer was gone. Divorce rates were rising. Sexual ethics were changing. Abortion clinics were opening. And behind it all was a fear: Has America turned its back on God?

The fear that once looked outward toward communism now turned inward, toward a perceived cultural collapse.

Fear is a major factor in decision making from a sociological perspective.[120] Fear shapes decisions. Fear manipulates nations. Fear sells faith. It functions not merely as a personal emotion but as a collective force that shapes how groups, communities, and even entire nations act. When fear spreads through a society, whether through economic uncertainty, threats of war, cultural change, or moral decline, it becomes a powerful motivator for collective behavior. People seek security, stability, and control, often turning to leaders, institutions, or ideologies that promise protection. In this sense, fear is not simply reactive; it is generative. It creates movements, molds policies, and establishes boundaries of what is considered acceptable or dangerous. And when fear becomes a strategy, it stops being holy.

Sociologists have long observed that fear exerts pressure toward conformity.[121] In moments of perceived crisis, individuals often align themselves with the majority or with authority figures, not necessarily because they are persuaded, but because they fear the cost of dissent. This was evident in the McCarthy era, when fear of communism silenced many voices, or during the Civil Rights Movement, when fear

---

[119] *Roe v. Wade*, 410 U.S. 113 (1973).

[120] Barry Glassner, The Culture of Fear: Why Americans Are Afraid of the Wrong Things (New York: Basic Books, 1999), xv–xvii.

[121] Émile Durkheim, *The Division of Labor in Society*, trans. George Simpson (New York: Free Press, 1933), 58–62; see also Stanley Cohen, *Folk Devils and Moral Panics* (London: Routledge, 1972), 27–30.

of social disruption caused many to resist change.[122] Fear narrows the range of options people are willing to consider, creating environments where decisions are less about conviction and more about survival. Fear narrows the current until only one channel remains: control.

Fear also serves as a political currency. Leaders and movements have historically leveraged fear, fear of outsiders, fear of moral collapse, fear of economic ruin, to mobilize followers and cement loyalty. When people believe their way of life is under threat, they are more likely to support drastic measures or surrender freedoms they would normally guard. This dynamic shows how fear shapes not only personal choices but also public policy and cultural narratives. In many ways, the "story of fear" is woven into the story of power. In every age, someone learns to profit from fear.

Yet fear is not always destructive. From a sociological angle, it can be seen as a protective mechanism that alerts societies to real dangers. Fear of disease, for example, can lead to improved public health practices. Fear of injustice can galvanize reform movements. The challenge comes in discerning whether fear is rooted in reality or in manipulation. Societies that fail to make this distinction risk being controlled by their fears rather than guided by their values.

In the mid-twentieth century, America felt that fog thickening. Rapid cultural shifts left many wondering if the moral foundations of the nation were being stripped away. News headlines about crime, protests, and rebellion only deepened the anxiety. For ordinary families, it wasn't simply politics; it was a fear that the country their children would inherit was slipping out of their control.

This fear didn't remain at the individual level. It became collective, and with it came a hunger for unity, for a rallying point strong enough to resist the tides of change. Politicians recognized its power, and some

---

122 Ellen Schrecker, Many Are the Crimes: McCarthyism in America (Boston: Little, Brown, 1998), 112–118.

preachers echoed it from the pulpit. Together, they began to frame the cultural upheaval not only as a political crisis but also as a spiritual one. The line between defending America and defending Christianity started to blur. Many Christians were deeply sincere, longing to protect their families from a changing world, but sincerity alone can't sanctify every response. The fog of fear often feels like faith when it promises safety.

Conservatives, both political and religious, saw an opportunity to join forces. Out of this crisis emerged what became known as the Religious Right.[123] The influence of this movement within American Christian history cannot be overstated. Many of today's senior leaders in politics, business, and institutions came of age in the Moral Majority era, which helps explain how deeply its assumptions still echo in public life.

In 1979, pastor Jerry Falwell (of Liberty University fame) founded the Moral Majority, a political organization that rallied conservative Christians into the political arena. [124] Falwell's Moral Majority galvanized believers around abortion, "family values," school prayer, resistance to the gay rights movement, and a strong defense posture.

Falwell argued that Christians could no longer remain passive. If America was drifting toward moral collapse, believers had to mobilize to preserve the nation's Christian heritage. These were noble aims, rooted in a desire for righteousness, and we'll explore them more deeply later. Yet at times, the Church's voice for morality grew louder than its voice for mercy.

The Moral Majority quickly became a powerful voting bloc. Millions of evangelicals who had once been politically disengaged were now casting ballots with new urgency.

---

[123] Randall Balmer, Bad Faith: Race and the Rise of the Religious Right (Grand Rapids, MI: Eerdmans, 2021), 41–45.

[124] Jerry Falwell, Listen, America! (Garden City, NY: Doubleday, 1980), 3–8; Susan Friend Hardman, Faith and Freedom: Jerry Falwell and the Rise of the Religious Right (Chapel Hill: University of North Carolina Press, 1987), 24–28.

The defining moment came with the election of Ronald Reagan in 1980.[125] Reagan courted the Religious Right openly, calling America a "shining city on a hill" and promising to restore its moral strength.[126]

Reagan spoke fluent faith-and-family. With his 1980 landslide, a quiet subculture became a decisive voting bloc. From then on, the word 'evangelical 'began to carry political connotations alongside its theological meaning.

Throughout the 1980s and beyond, the Religious Right shaped American politics in profound ways[127]:

- Pro-life movement: abortion became the central issue binding evangelicals to conservatism.
- Family values: promoting traditional moral standards and opposing cultural changes related to sexuality and gender roles.
- Education battles: defending Christian schools and homeschooling against federal oversight.
- Patriotism and defense: linking Christianity with American strength against communism.

The Religious Right often framed these issues as more than political debates, as spiritual battles between faith and secularism.

The rise of the Religious Right was not without fruit: civic engagement, moral questions back in national view, and enduring networks of churches, schools, and media.

---

125 Ronald Reagan, "Acceptance Address at the Republican National Convention," July 17, 1980, *Public Papers of the Presidents of the United States* (Washington, DC: GPO, 1980), 1048–1052.

126 Ronald Reagan, "Farewell Address to the Nation," January 11, 1989, *Public Papers of the Presidents of the United States* (Washington, DC: GPO, 1989), 1724.

127 Daniel K. Williams, *God s Own Party: The Making of the Christian Right* (New York: Oxford University Press, 2010), 145–150.

It brought conviction, but also confusion about the source of true power. But the movement also carried deep risks: partisanship eclipsing discipleship, culture-war rhetoric drowning out the gospel of peace, moral double standards for "our side," and the alienation of many Christians of color and non-evangelical traditions.

Every alliance carries a cost, and this one tested the Church's identity.

In defending Christianity's place in America, the Church risked losing its purpose in the Kingdom.

By the 1990s, the Religious Right had become a permanent force in American politics.[128] Even when the Moral Majority itself faded, its legacy lived on in groups like the Christian Coalition, Focus on the Family, and a vast network of media outlets and advocacy groups.[129]

The fusion of Christianity and conservatism was no longer just cultural, it was institutional. Churches became political mobilizers. Evangelical identity became increasingly defined by party affiliation.[130]

And yet, beneath the surface, the question lingered:

Was this truly advancing The River of Life, or simply preserving The Current of America?

The rise of the Moral Majority and the Religious Right marked a turning point in American history.[131] No longer content to be a moral backdrop, Christianity became a political force. Evangelicals, once seen

---

[128] Clyde Wilcox, Onward Christian Soldiers? The Religious Right in American Politics (Boulder, CO: Westview Press, 1992), 3–6.

[129] Ralph Reed, Active Faith: How Christians Are Changing the Soul of American Politics (New York: Free Press, 1996), 11–14.

[130] Robert P. Jones, *The End of White Christian America* (New York: Simon & Schuster, 2016), 58–61.

[131] Mark A. Noll, *The Scandal of the Evangelical Mind* (Grand Rapids, MI: Eerdmans, 1994), 110–113.

as a quiet subculture, became a decisive power in national elections. Discipleship takes a lifetime; movements want results by November.

But with this influence came danger: the risk of confusing the eternal Kingdom of Christ with the temporary kingdoms of men. The Religious Right sought to save America, but sometimes lost sight of the greater mission, to make disciples of all nations. The Church had perfected the assembly line, mass-producing believers faster than it could mature them. At times, we defended values we struggled to live out, and condemned sins we privately wrestled with

This chapter of history leaves modern Christians with a haunting question: What happens when faith is so closely tied to politics that people can no longer tell them apart?

The Church lost something in those years: not its relevance, but its reverence.[132] And now, decades later, we must ask ourselves: Did we gain influence at the cost of intimacy? Did we win the culture and lose the Kingdom? Because the river that once flowed freely through prayer and humility grew obstructed by politics and pride. And if we want to see it flow again, we'll have to stop fighting for control and start falling to our knees. Revival doesn't start in a voting booth. It starts in a broken heart.[133] The only way to free The River of Life again is repentance.

🕮 REFLECTION QUESTIONS

1. What motivated evangelicals to enter politics so forcefully in the 1970s and 80s?
2. What good came from the Religious Right, and what dangers did it create for the church's witness?

---

[132] Philip Yancey, *What s So Amazing About Grace?* (Grand Rapids, MI: Zondervan, 1997), 19–22.

[133] 2 Chronicles 7:14 (New International Version).

3. How can Christians today engage in politics without repeating the mistakes of the Moral Majority?

Chapter Nine

THE SUMMER OF '69 AND THE SEEDS OF PANIC

One of my all-time favorite films is 'Once Upon a Time in Hollywood.' I don't love the language or violence, but I love the story. My wife and I are borderline obsessed with "Old Hollywood" and love that time period. The film is a reimagined history that tells the story of a stunt man who helps his actor friend take down the Manson family before they ever murdered Sharon Tate. If only that were the true history.

Tarantino imagines evil stopped before it starts. Real 1969 didn't end that way. That summer became shorthand for a nation searching for freedom, and finding both ecstasy and emptiness. It marked one of the major turning points in American history; one that warrants a closer look in this chapter.

The late 1960s marked one of the most dramatic cultural shifts in American history. The year 1969 in particular became symbolic of a new world, one that unsettled conservatives and challenged the moral authority of the church.

That summer saw:

- Woodstock: 400,000 young people gathered for three days of music, sex, drugs, and countercultural rebellion.[134]
- The Sexual Revolution: "free love" was preached as liberation from traditional morality.[135]
- Drug Culture: LSD, marijuana, and psychedelic experimentation moved from fringe to mainstream.[136]
- The Manson Murders: Charles Manson and his cult horrified the nation, showing how spiritual rebellion could turn violent.[137]
- The Moon Landing: technological triumph mingled with social chaos, symbolizing both human progress and cultural upheaval.[138]

The same summer that promised freedom also began to redefine it. Beneath the music and the marches, the moral foundations of the nation began to shift. *The Current of Culture* that once carried dreams of unity split into tributaries of rebellion and self-expression, and the waters grew wild.

To many Americans, this wasn't just cultural change, it was moral collapse. For Christians, it felt like an open rebellion against God.

Conservatives, both political and religious, saw the summer of '69 as proof that America was drifting dangerously away from its roots.

---

134 Michael Lang, *The Road to Woodstock* (New York: Ecco, 2009), 3–8.

135 Jeffrey Escoffier, *Sexual Revolution* (New York: Oxford University Press, 2003), 15–22.

136 Martin A. Lee and Bruce Shlain, Acid Dreams: The Complete Social History of LSD: The CIA, the Sixties, and Beyond (New York: Grove Press, 1985), 94–99.

137 Vincent Bugliosi and Curt Gentry, Helter Skelter: The True Story of the Manson Murders (New York: W. W. Norton, 1974), 17–24.

138 Robert Poole, *Earthrise: How Man First Saw the Earth* (New Haven, CT: Yale University Press, 2008), 132–136.

Rock music became a target, accused of promoting drugs, sex, and even occultism.

Many in mainstream America caricatured hippies as reckless and threatening to family stability.

The breakdown of traditional sexual norms and rising divorce rates fed the sense that America was under real attack, not by an enemy abroad, but by a cultural revolution at home.

To many, this wasn't mere change, it was rebellion. Rock was suspect; hippies were reckless, marriage felt fragile. "Law and order" migrated from stump speeches to sermons.

Out of this cultural upheaval grew a heightened fear of the demonic.[139] Several factors converged:

- The popularity of horror films like Rosemary's Baby (1968) and The Exorcist (1973) blurred entertainment with spiritual dread.[140]
- Rumors and reports of cult activity, real or exaggerated, fueled the sense that Satan was literally on the march.
- Rock bands like Led Zeppelin, Black Sabbath, and later heavy metal groups were accused of hiding occult symbols in their music.

By the late 1970s, anxiety hardened into the Satanic Panic[141]:

- Sensational daycare-abuse claims later discredited
- Backmasking scares about hidden messages in rock

---

139 Philip Jenkins, Mystics and Messiahs: Cults and New Religions in American History (New York: Oxford University Press, 2000), 203–210.

140 Rosemary Guiley, The Encyclopedia of Demons and Demonology (New York: Facts On File, 2009), 89–92.

141 Jeffrey S. Victor, Satanic Panic: The Creation of a Contemporary Legend (Chicago: Open Court, 1993), 1–4.

- Moral alarms around Dungeons & Dragons

Fear began to frame culture as a cosmic invasion, and politics as potential deliverance.[142] It wasn't just the devil people feared, it was losing control of a world they no longer understood.

Though little evidence ever substantiated these claims, the fear was real, and politically useful.[143] It galvanized Christians to see themselves in a cosmic struggle for the soul of the nation.

For many evangelicals, the cultural collapse of the late 60s and the rise of the Satanic Panic confirmed their worldview: America was not just in decline, but under spiritual attack. But fear, once baptized, rarely stays pure.

Churches doubled down on preaching against sex, drugs, and rock & roll.

Youth ministries were built around "rescuing" kids from cultural corruption. Rather than letting *The River of Life* flow freely into a searching culture, we sometimes built walls of defensiveness. The Church at times seemed to forget that holiness is not the same as hostility. It preached morality without mercy, and truth without tenderness. Jesus touched lepers while we built fences.

Many evangelicals came to see political conservatism as a primary defense against what they perceived as moral chaos. *The Current* of America narrowed again, channeled into a single partisan stream.

The panic may have exaggerated threats, but it effectively mobilized Christians into cultural engagement. Fear is a powerful evangelist when hope grows quiet.

---

142 Paul Boyer, When Time Shall Be No More: Prophecy Belief in Modern American Culture (Cambridge, MA: Harvard University Press, 1992), 268–272.

143 Richard Beck, We Believe the Children: A Moral Panic in the 1980s (New York: PublicAffairs, 2015), 14–18.

And yet, amid the chaos, revival flickered; the Jesus Movement drew thousands to simple, Spirit-led faith. Confusion and renewal often share a decade.[144]

The Summer of '69 and the Satanic Panic created a narrative that still shapes conservative Christianity today.

It led many Christians to believe that culture was not just morally weak but spiritually under siege. That change itself was war. That the gospel must go to battle or be buried.

This narrative became the foundation for the Religious Right in the 1980s and beyond.

The Summer of '69 was not just a cultural turning point, it was a spiritual turning point in America's imagination. What some saw as freedom, others saw as rebellion. What some celebrated as progress, others feared as decline. Out of this tension grew a generation of Christians who saw politics and culture not just as issues to debate, but as battlegrounds of cosmic significance. It was a moment when America often stopped asking "What is true?" and began asking "Whose side are you on?"

The Satanic Panic may have exaggerated threats, but it left behind a deeper conviction: that conservatism and Christianity must join forces to protect America from collapse. Whether that conviction was faithful or fearful is a question that still challenges the church today.

The River was still flowing, but the Church no longer trusted its depth. The Spirit was still moving, but we were too busy guarding our shores. We tested the water instead of trusting the source.

For the first time, the *Current of the Culture* seemed to split in two. One current surged forward, chasing progress, liberation, and self-

144 Larry Eskridge, God's Forever Family: The Jesus People Movement in America (New York: Oxford University Press, 2013), 55–60.

expression. The other recoiled, fearful, disoriented, clinging to the riverbanks of a world that suddenly felt unrecognizable.

To many believers, it felt like the world had come unanchored. The prayers once heard in classrooms were replaced with Beatles lyrics.[145] Marriage, once sacred, seemed fragile. The Church had once felt like it was steering the ship; now it often found itself clinging to the sides, unsure of the tide.

For a brief moment, America looked heavenward. The astronauts read Scripture from space, families prayed before televisions, and the words, "In the beginning, God created" echoed across the airwaves.[146] But even that moment of wonder faded as the counterculture found a new religion, self. Even as man walked on the moon, he began to forget how to walk with God.[147]

Peace signs replaced crosses. Personal freedom replaced moral order. And by the end of the decade, even those who had celebrated change began to sense something hollow in the air.

The Summer of '69 became a symbol, of both promise and panic.[148] It revealed a nation yearning for transcendence but allergic to authority. We wanted heaven without holiness. Progress without repentance. And somewhere in that confusion, the Church's fear took root.

Parents worried they were losing their children. Pastors worried they were losing the culture. Politicians promised they could bring it all

---

145 Mark Lewisohn, The Beatles: All These Years, Vol. 1 – Tune In (New York: Crown Archetype, 2013), 612–618.

146 Genesis 1:1–10 (King James Version); see also *NASA Apollo 8 Mission Transcript*, December 24, 1968, NASA History Office Archives.

147 Andrew Root, *Faith Formation in a Secular Age* (Grand Rapids, MI: Baker Academic, 2017), 44–46.

148 David Farber, The Age of Great Dreams: America in the 1960s (New York: Hill and Wang, 1994), 187–192.

back. Thus began a new movement, A movement born more from reaction than revival.

The moral panic of the '60s and '70s soon took the stage, singing hymns of fear, waving flags of faith, sometimes mistaking control for conviction. It would march under banners of righteousness, believing they were defending God Himself. But fear and faith can't share the same throne.

And whenever the Church builds from panic rather than prayer, *The River of Life* slows to a crawl. Because revival never begins in reaction to culture, it begins in repentance before Christ.

🕮 REFLECTION QUESTIONS

1. How did the cultural upheaval of the 1960s shape the fears of conservative Christians?
2. Why do you think the Satanic Panic was so powerful, even when much of it was unfounded?
3. What lessons can the church learn today about responding to cultural change with faith rather than fear?

Chapter Ten

TWISTING THE SACRED TEXT, HOW MISREADING SCRIPTURE SHAPED A NATION

Before we move into the 21st century, it's worth pausing to take a side road, to explore one of the most destructive and misunderstood patterns in our nation's story: how *The River of Life*'s Word, when diverted from its context, can become a weapon instead of a witness.

The Bible is a double-edged sword, and when handled without humility, it can wound in the wrong direction. It has set captives free and comforted the brokenhearted. But history also shows that when Scripture is lifted out of context, it has been used to bind the vulnerable and to justify oppression. The same Word that once parted seas can, in human hands, be misused in ways that harden hearts.

At various points in our history, Scripture has been bent toward three ends: to justify, to sanctify, and to weaponize.

1. To Justify Our Desires

When people crave legitimacy, they reach for the sacred. Slaveholders quoted Paul's household codes to defend bondage. [149] Politicians invoked divine favor to defend expansion.[150] Some Christians cited Romans 13 in ways that effectively baptized nationalism. But every time we read the Bible to affirm our behavior instead of transform it, we drift from being disciples toward becoming editors. The Word of God was never meant to defend our way of life, it was meant to define it. When we stop letting Scripture confront us, we start recruiting it.

2. To Sanctify Our Systems

After justification comes sanctification, the illusion that success is proof of divine blessing. When the Industrial Age flourished, sermons on diligence sometimes eclipsed sermons on dependence. When capitalism prospered, prosperity theology followed close behind.[151]We forgot that blessing in Scripture is always tied to burden, to generosity, to justice, to grace. Jesus warned that we cannot serve both God and money. But we tried. We sometimes tried to build temples to both and called it balance. The result? A nation that still sings about God's grace while trusting in its own grind. We often confused fruitfulness with fortune.

3. To Weaponize Our Faith

Perhaps the most painful twist came when the Bible became ammunition. Verses meant to comfort were sometimes turned into ammunition that condemned those who were different. Truth became a weapon instead of a wound-healer. The gospel began to sound more

149 Mark Noll, *The Civil War as a Theological Crisis* (Chapel Hill: University of North Carolina Press, 2006), 22–25.

150 Albert K. Weinberg, Manifest Destiny: A Study of Nationalist Expansion in American History (Baltimore: Johns Hopkins University Press, 1935), 54–56.

151 Kate Bowler, Blessed: A History of the American Prosperity Gospel (New York: Oxford University Press, 2013), 41–47.

like an argument than an announcement But the Word was never meant to win debates. It was meant to resurrect the dead. It was never meant to silence our opponents but to invite them to salvation.

Nowhere is that tension more visible than in the American story, where the Word of God was invoked to bless ambition, baptize racism, and consecrate violence, all under the banner of divine will.

We have to wrestle honestly with this truth: many of our nation's sins were committed while Scripture was invoked

When John L. O'Sullivan coined the phrase Manifest Destiny in 1845, he clothed westward expansion in spiritual language: "It is our manifest destiny," he wrote, "to overspread the continent allotted by Providence."[152]

That word, Providence, sacred and sobering, gave settlers permission to believe that their ambition was God's anointing. America wasn't just expanding; it was fulfilling God's plan.

Politicians and pastors preached from texts like Genesis 1:28, "Be fruitful and multiply, fill the earth and subdue it," as if it were a license again, channeled to claim the land rather than care for it.[153] The language of "subduing" creation was torn from its original context of stewardship and transformed into a theology of domination. The call to stewardship was too often recast as permission for conquest.

In pulpits, the story of ancient Israel became America's story. The wilderness became the new Canaan. Settlers were the "new Israelites." And those who already lived on the land, Indigenous nations who had

---

[152] John L. O'Sullivan, "Annexation," United States Magazine and Democratic Review 17 (July–August 1845): 5–10.

[153] Robert E. Shaw, American Patriotic Protestantism: National Faith and Manifest Destiny, 1800–1860 (New York: Garland Publishing, 1985), 89–92.

cultivated it for centuries, were cast as "Canaanites" standing in the way of God's promise.

The result was a faith that at times confused calling with conquest.

Few moments reveal this distortion more painfully than the Trail of Tears.[154]

Between 1830 and 1850, over 60,000 Native Americans, Cherokee, Muscogee, Seminole, Chickasaw, and Choctaw, were forced from their ancestral lands, marched hundreds of miles to what's now Oklahoma. Thousands died from starvation, disease, and exposure. The trail wasn't just marked by footprints, but by verses misused and promises betrayed.

President Andrew Jackson, a professing Christian, defended the Indian Removal Act as a benevolent plan.[155] He claimed it would "save" Native peoples from extinction by moving them westward. "It will place a dense and civilized population in large tracts of country now occupied by a few savage hunters," he wrote. It reflected a gospel of uniformity rather than unity, a creed leaning toward control more than compassion.

"Civilized." That word carried the weight of a false gospel, one that confused assimilation with salvation. Missionaries, too, often participated in the deception, teaching that conversion required cultural erasure.

Scripture was used as justification. Settlers pointed to Deuteronomy 7, where God commands Israel to drive out the nations before them,

---

[154] Claudio Saunt, Unworthy Republic: The Dispossession of Native Americans and the Road to Indian Territory (New York: W. W. Norton, 2020), 103–110.

[155] Andrew Jackson, *Second Annual Message to Congress, December 6, 1830*, in *The Papers of Andrew Jackson*, vol. 8, ed. Daniel Feller et al. (Knoxville: University of Tennessee Press, 2010), 245–248.

ignoring that this was a unique command tied to Israel's covenant with God, not a universal mandate for any nation to conquer another.

The Trail of Tears wasn't just a national tragedy. It was a theological one. It revealed what happens when The River of Life is rerouted through the channels of power.

A century earlier, the same misreading had already poisoned the nation's soul. Slaveholders quoted the Bible as their defense:

- "Slaves, obey your masters." (Ephesians 6:5)
- If a slave has taken refuge with you, do not hand them over to their master." (Deuteronomy 23:15–16), conveniently ignored.

Pro-slavery preachers in the South insisted that slavery was divinely ordained. Reverend Thornton Stringfellow, in his infamous 1856 pamphlet A Scriptural View of Slavery, argued that God Himself had instituted slavery through Noah and Abraham.[156] He claimed it was "a relation of mutual kindness," ordained for the good of both races.

Few distortions were more grievous than this. The very gospel that proclaims liberation from bondage was used to justify bondage itself.

It is important to note this. It's easy to condemn such distortion now, but every age faces fresh temptations to twist verses in its favor

On the flip side, abolitionists like Frederick Douglass and Harriet Beecher Stowe read the same Bible and found a very different message: a God who hears the cry of the oppressed and sets captives free.[157] "Between the Christianity of this land and the Christianity of Christ,"

---

156 Thornton Stringfellow, *A Scriptural View of Slavery* (Richmond: J. W. Randolph, 1856), 3–9.

157 Frederick Douglass, *Narrative of the Life of Frederick Douglass, an American Slave* (Boston: Anti-Slavery Office, 1845), 118; Harriet Beecher Stowe, *Uncle Tom s Cabin* (Boston: John P. Jewett, 1852), 7–10.

Douglass wrote, "I recognize the widest possible difference." The same ink that once justified chains was also used to pen freedom's cry.

The issue was never the Bible itself, it was how it was read. When we read for power, we tend to find justification; when we read for justice, we are drawn toward Jesus.

By 1861, America's divide was not just political; it was theological.[158] Both sides claimed God was on their side. Confederate soldiers marched to war singing "God Will Defend the Right." Union soldiers sang "Mine eyes have seen the glory of the coming of the Lord." The Bible became both battlefield and banner.

The same Scripture was interpreted through opposing lenses: one emphasizing hierarchy, the other emphasizing deliverance. The war became a clash between two readings of the same sacred text, one that upheld hierarchy, and one that sought equality.

President Abraham Lincoln, in his Second Inaugural Address, acknowledged the irony:

"Both read the same Bible and pray to the same God, and each invokes His aid against the other The prayers of both could not be answered."[159]

In that moment, Lincoln did what few leaders had done before: he humbled the nation before the Word, rather than using the Word to sanctify the nation. Lincoln's humility remains a rare moment when Scripture was allowed to search us rather than simply support us.

---

158 Harry S. Stout, Upon the Altar of the Nation: A Moral History of the Civil War (New York: Viking, 2006), 115–118.

159 Abraham Lincoln, *Second Inaugural Address*, March 4, 1865, in *Collected Works of Abraham Lincoln*, vol. 8, ed. Roy P. Basler (New Brunswick, NJ: Rutgers University Press, 1953), 332.

After the war, as Reconstruction faltered and Jim Crow laws emerged, America found itself again torn between two gospels, the gospel of Christ and the gospel of culture.

The Bible was quoted to defend segregation.[160] White pastors argued that God "separated the races" in Babel and commanded them not to mix. Black pastors, meanwhile, preached Exodus, "Let my people go." One reading reinforced pews of privilege; another helped build paths to freedom.

The Civil Rights Movement of the 1950s and '60s became, in many ways, a battle over who was interpreting Scripture faithfully.

Dr. Martin Luther King Jr., in his *Letter from Birmingham Jail*, addressed white clergymen who had accused him of disturbing the peace.[161] He replied:

"I have almost reached the regrettable conclusion that the Negro's great stumbling block is not the White Citizen's Councilor or the Ku Klux Klanner, but the white moderate who is more devoted to 'order 'than to justice Shallow understanding from people of good will is more frustrating than absolute misunderstanding from people of ill will."

King's reading of Scripture, shaped by the prophets and the teachings of Jesus, stood in stark contrast to those who used the Bible to maintain comfort and control. King read Scripture through the prophets and the teachings of Jesus, and helped the nation rediscover it.

The same book. Two readings. One builds bridges; the other builds barriers.

---

160 David L. Chappell, *A Stone of Hope: Prophetic Religion and the Death of Jim Crow* (Chapel Hill: University of North Carolina Press, 2004), 49–54.

161 Martin Luther King Jr., *Letter from Birmingham Jail* (April 16, 1963), in *Why We Can t Wait* (New York: Harper & Row, 1964), 77–79.

The temptation to weaponize Scripture didn't end with slavery or segregation. We still face this temptation today, to quote verses as proof texts for our opinions rather than invitations to repentance.

We quote 2 Chronicles 7:14 as if America were Israel, but forget that God's people are now defined by faith, not nationality.[162] We post Jeremiah 29:11 for prosperity but ignore the verses about exile and repentance. We celebrate "If God is for us, who can be against us?" without remembering that Paul wrote those words from prison.[163] We love promises of healing, but not the prerequisite of humility.

When the church forgets context, division follows. When we read the Bible to confirm our biases, we lose the power to confront them.

The Word of God was never meant to serve our agendas; it was meant to expose them.

The misuse of Scripture has caused untold damage, from the Trail of Tears to slavery to segregation, but that same Scripture, rightly read, still holds the power to heal. The antidote to twisted Scripture is humble reading, Scripture interpreted through the self-emptying lens of Christ rather than the self-preserving lens of culture.

It reminds us that all people are made in the image of God.[164] That justice and mercy are inseparable. That the gospel isn't about a chosen nation, but a redeemed creation.

When we approach Scripture with humility, letting it read us before we read it, the sword that once wounded can begin to heal.

If we are to heal as a nation and as the Church, we must repent not only of what we did with Scripture, but of how we used it. We must

---

162 2 Chronicles 7:14 (New International Version).
163 Romans 8:31 (New International Version).
164 Genesis 1:27 (New International Version).

rediscover context, wrestle with history, and listen to the voices we once silenced.

True biblical faith doesn't make us proud; it makes us humble. It doesn't draw lines in the sand; it washes feet. True faith doesn't win arguments; it wins hearts.

When the church returns to that kind of reading, when we allow Scripture to dismantle our idols of nationalism, race, and power, we might finally live up to the words we so often quote: "You will know the truth, and the truth will set you free."[165] (John 8:32) Because when truth runs freely, it becomes a river again, cutting through stone, cleansing what's been polluted.

If the Bible has been misused to divide, it can also be rediscovered to unite. The same Word that was once twisted to justify oppression can still speak healing into a broken land.

But it begins with humility, with the courage to say:

"We misread it. We misused it. And by God's grace, we won't do it again."

We've all done it, quoted Scripture to win an argument, defend a position, or soothe our pride. But the Bible is not a mirror for our opinions. It's a window into God's heart. And when we hold it up only to see ourselves, we stop seeing Him.

The same Spirit who inspired Scripture is the only one who can interpret it rightly. Without His guidance, we weaponize what was meant to heal and misrepresent the One we claim to follow. God's Word is not a tool for power but a testimony of love. It does not bend to our agendas; it breaks them open. It does not flow through systems of control; it flows from the throne of grace. If we want revival in our

---

[165] John 8:32 (New International Version).

nation, it won't come from quoting the Bible louder; it will come from living it deeper.

Because the truth was never meant to make us superior. It was meant to make us surrender.

🕮 Reflection Questions

1. Before reading this chapter, how familiar were you with the concept of Manifest Destiny? How does seeing its theological justifications change the way you understand American history?
2. What are some examples from the chapter where Scripture was taken out of context to justify injustice (e.g., westward expansion, slavery, segregation)?
3. Have you ever found yourself using Scripture to validate your own opinion, lifestyle, or worldview instead of letting Scripture challenge it? What did that look like?
4. Why do you think it's easier to pull verses out of context than to study the full story around them?
5. How can the Church today guard against the same mistakes that fueled Manifest Destiny, using Scripture to defend power instead of reveal truth?

Chapter Eleven

THE 21ST CENTURY FUSION

I was in the third grade in music class with Mrs. Spangler. We were singing a choral version of the song called "Heal The World" by Michael Jackson. I remember another teacher knocking on the door in tears. Everything after that was kind of a blur. Mrs. Spangler wheeled in the TV cart and turned on the news. We watched in horror. My dad came to pick me up and bring me home. My church met that night and held hands and prayed. People cried. People mourned. People were angry and afraid. That day, everything changed.

On September 11, 2001, smoke rose over New York and with it the nation's prayers. [166] Churches filled. Pastors spoke of judgment, repentance, and renewal. Politicians invoked God and destiny. For a moment, The River of Life seemed to surge to the surface and mingle with The Current of America.

This was a cultural turning point that helped shape the current of the cultural river in ways that had been unrivaled in decades.

---

166 Robert Bellah et al., Habits of the Heart: Individualism and Commitment in American Life (Berkeley: University of California Press, 2008), 267–70.

It often felt as though the line between faith and patriotism had dissolved. To many, being American felt synonymous with being a believer; resisting America felt like resisting God. Flags filled sanctuaries, and sermons sounded more like speeches.

For evangelicals especially, 9/11 reinforced the belief that the United States was engaged in a cosmic struggle between good and evil.[167] But beneath that unity, something deeper was forming: a fusion of Christianity and conservatism that would shape the identity of the church for decades. In the smoke of Ground Zero, the Church faced an ancient temptation, to confuse divine mission with national defense.

President George W. Bush seemed tailor-made for this moment.[168] A man who had spoken openly about his personal conversion, how faith in Christ delivered him from alcoholism, Bush embodied the blend of politics and testimony that evangelicals longed for. Faith and politics, once cautious partners, began to feel like family

In his speeches, Bush frequently used biblical imagery: "evil-doers," "light in the darkness," "freedom as God's gift." [169] For many evangelicals, this language felt like reassurance that someone in the White House understood them.

During the Bush administration, for example:

- Faith-based initiatives gave federal funds to religious charities.[170]
- Pro-life policies were strengthened.

---

[167] Andrew Preston, Sword of the Spirit, Shield of Faith: Religion in American War and Diplomacy (New York: Knopf, 2012), 582–86.

[168] George W. Bush, *Decision Points* (New York: Crown, 2010), 67–72.

[169] George W. Bush, "Address to a Joint Session of Congress and the American People," September 20, 2001, *The American Presidency Project*, accessed October 2025, https://www.presidency.ucsb.edu.

[170] John J. DiIulio Jr., Godly Republic: A Centrist Blueprint for America's Faith-Based Future (Berkeley: University of California Press, 2007), 33–38.

- National defense was cast in moral and spiritual terms.

For many Christians, Bush wasn't just their president; he was their brother in Christ. The fusion deepened for many.

But as evangelicals felt emboldened politically, cultural shifts seemed to accelerate.

Same-sex marriage gained momentum, culminating in Obergefell v. Hodges (2015), which legalized it nationwide.[171] While some churches gained influence, the broader culture accelerated, often in different directions.

Abortion battles raged in state legislatures and the Supreme Court.

Media and entertainment increasingly normalized values that clashed with conservative Christian beliefs.

These developments weren't simply seen as cultural disagreements, they were framed as spiritual battles. Churches preached about the "war on the family." Conservative commentators warned of America's moral collapse.

By the mid-2000s, the phrase "culture war" was no longer a metaphor. For many evangelicals, it described reality.

The election of Barack Obama in 2008 brought hope for many Americans, but for much of evangelical conservatism, it deepened the sense of siege.[172] For many conservatives, Obama's policies on life and sexuality confirmed a story of national drift. For others, his election embodied overdue hope. The same event told profoundly different stories.

---

[171] *Obergefell v. Hodges*, 576 U.S. 644 (2015).

[172] Michael Eric Dyson, The Black Presidency: Barack Obama and the Politics of Race in America (Boston: Houghton Mifflin Harcourt, 2016), 112–15.

Every river, when dammed too long, finds a way to rush again. The next surge came in the form of change.

Some evangelicals embraced conspiracy claims, questioning Obama's religion or even his birthplace. [173] These weren't just political suspicions; they reflected a deeper spiritual anxiety: If Obama represents America's future, then the church has already lost. When fear replaces faith, discernment tends to drown.

During the Obama years, the fusion of conservatism and Christianity became more defensive. Many evangelicals shifted from asking how to shape culture to asking how to endure in a culture they no longer recognized.

Then came Donald Trump. As Israel once begged for a king, many in the Church longed for a fighter.[174]

On paper, Donald Trump seemed an unlikely evangelical champion: brash, wealthy, profane, with a history of affairs and divorces. Yet in 2016, he won over evangelical voters by overwhelming margins. Why?

- Because Trump positioned himself as a fighter.
- He promised conservative judges who would finally overturn Roe v. Wade.
- He vowed to protect religious liberty, even calling Christians "the most persecuted group in America."
- He attacked 'elites,' 'fake news, 'and progressive agendas in ways that echoed frustrations many evangelicals felt.
- He framed himself not as a saint, but as a warrior sent to defend Christians in a hostile land.

---

[173] John S. Fea, Believe Me: The Evangelical Road to Donald Trump (Grand Rapids, MI: Eerdmans, 2018), 41–45.

[174] Kristin Kobes Du Mez, Jesus and John Wayne: How White Evangelicals Corrupted a Faith and Fractured a Nation (New York: Liveright, 2020), 181–84.

For many evangelicals, Trump became a paradoxical symbol: personally immoral, but politically indispensable. Like King Cyrus of Persia, who unwittingly blessed Israel, Trump was seen not as holy, but as useful.[175] And for some, perceived usefulness began to resemble anointing. Many believers, drawing on Cyrus analogies, took political usefulness for divine endorsement.

To many observers, the fusion now looked complete, Christianity and conservatism nearly indistinguishable.

The 21st century saw an explosion of conservative-Christian institutions.[176] With political revival came media revival, another kind of pulpit, and for some, another kind of preacher.

- Fox News and later conservative media platforms became quasi-religious authorities for many believers.
- The Tea Party movement linked fiscal conservatism with religious conservatism, expanding evangelical influence.
- Social media amplified culture wars, with Facebook and Twitter becoming battlegrounds where Christians often echoed partisan talking points more than Scripture.
- Megachurches and celebrity pastors sometimes became political platforms, hosting candidates and shaping voter blocs.

Christianity was not just engaged with politics, it was saturated in it.

The Trump era also saw the rise of conspiracy-driven movements like QAnon, which fused end-times prophecy, patriotism, and internet

---

[175] Thomas Kidd, Who Is an Evangelical? The History of a Movement in Crisis (New Haven: Yale University Press, 2019), 153–56.

[176] Mark A. Noll and George Marsden, Evangelicals and Civic Life: Public Religion in America (New York: Oxford University Press, 2019), 212–16.

mythology into a new kind of folk religion.[177] Some Christians began interpreting QAnon through the lens of biblical prophecy, blending eschatology with political conspiracy. Theology became threaded with hashtags; prophecy sometimes tangled with paranoia.

This was the extreme fruit of the fusion: politics not only informed faith, but replaced it in some hearts.

To be fair, the conservative-Christian alliance achieved real results:

- The overturning of Roe v. Wade in 2022, the result of decades of prayer, activism, and judicial appointments.[178]
- Expanded protections for religious liberty in schools, businesses, and institutions.
- Prayer met policy, and persistence bore fruit.
- Mobilization of millions of believers to take faith seriously in every sphere of life.

For many evangelicals, these victories justified the political compromises.

But the costs have been heavy:

- Credibility lost: The church became known more for its politics than for the gospel.
- Division deepened: Congregations split over politics, sometimes more fiercely than over theology.
- Generations alienated: Many younger believers grew weary of culture-war framing and left churches at higher rates. Surveys consistently show that Millennials and Gen Z see Christianity as hypocritical, angry, and politically obsessed.[179]

---

177 Samuel L. Perry, Andrew L. Whitehead, and Joshua B. Grubbs, The Flag and the Cross: Christian Nationalism and the Threat to American Democracy (New York: Oxford University Press, 2022), 94–99.

178 Dobbs v. Jackson Women's Health Organization, 597 U.S. 215 (2022).

179 Barna Group, "The State of the Church 2023," Barna.com, accessed October 2025, https://www.barna.com/research/state-of-the-church-2023.

- Witness obscured: At times, the church's prophetic voice was eclipsed by a partisan echo.

In trying to save America, we lost something of the gospel's accent. The fusion has delivered short-term influence but may risk long-term credibility.

From the outside, Christianity in America is often perceived not as a faith, but as a political movement. Global Christians, especially in the persecuted church, look at the American church with confusion: Why tie the gospel of Christ to one political leader or party?[180] Why risk credibility for temporary victories? Jesus asked, 'What good is it to gain the whole world and forfeit your soul? '(Mark 8:36).[181] The modern church might ask the same of its witness. More people began asking not what we believe, but whom we voted for.

The fusion has made it harder for outsiders to see Jesus clearly.

The 21st century fusion has left the American church at a crossroads:

Will we continue to define our faith by political victories?

Or will we rediscover a Kingdom identity that transcends politics?

If the church chooses the first path, it may win elections but lose its witness. If it chooses the second, it may lose power but regain credibility.

The Current of partisanship is strong, but *The River of Life* is stronger. One builds walls; the other washes feet. The river feels split again, one current pulling toward power, another toward purity.

The choice is stark, but clear: Are we building Christ's Kingdom, or America's kingdom? Somewhere along the way, we stopped asking,

---

[180] Philip Jenkins, *The Next Christendom: The Coming of Global Christianity*, 3rd ed. (New York: Oxford University Press, 2011), 223–28.

[181] Mark 8:36 (New International Version).

"What does Jesus say?" and started asking, "What does my side believe?" Faith became another layer of brand loyalty, red or blue, urban or rural, progressive or conservative.

Our creeds too easily turned into hashtags, and our unity thinned into factions. We no longer worshiped around the cross; we gathered behind our causes. And in the process, we sometimes traded the Kingdom for a camp. But the Kingdom of God doesn't fly our colors. It flies the banner of a crucified King. He doesn't fit in our categories, He overturns them. Whenever faith fuses too tightly with tribe, it risks losing its power to transform.

The fusion can feel unstoppable. But fires that burn too hot eventually consume themselves. And when the smoke clears, what remains will be what has always been, the unchanging river of Christ's love, still flowing quietly beneath the chaos. Even when the surface burns, the river beneath still runs cool.

He's calling us to de-fuse our faith, to separate what is cultural from what is holy, what is loud from what is lasting.

The early Church didn't change the world by winning arguments. It changed the world by living differently.[182] They didn't dam the river, they dived into it. That's still the invitation today.

Because fusion may define our age, but formation will define our eternity. And the only way to move against this current is to return to the Source Himself.

---

182 Rodney Stark, The Rise of Christianity: How the Obscure, Marginal Jesus Movement Became the Dominant Religious Force in the Western World in a Few Centuries (Princeton, NJ: Princeton University Press, 1996), 195–98.

🕮 REFLECTION QUESTIONS

1. What role did fear play in binding evangelicals to conservative politics after 9/11 and during Obama's presidency?
2. Why do you think so many evangelicals embraced Trump despite his lifestyle?
3. How has social media shaped the fusion of Christianity and conservatism?
4. What do you think younger generations are rejecting when they leave the church, Jesus Himself, or the fusion of Jesus with politics?
5. If Christianity were disentangled from conservatism, what would it look like in America today?

Chapter Twelve

CULTURAL TOUCHPOINTS OF THE FUSION

Ideas move slowly. But events, narratives, celebrities, and symbols move fast. For many Christians in America, the fusion of faith and conservatism hasn't just been a theology; it's been lived in high-visibility moments. These cultural touchpoints serve as shaping stories, they teach people what it means to belong, who is friend or foe, and how faith and politics intertwine. Like stones thrown into a river, these moments send ripples far beyond their origin.

If Chapter 11 painted the panorama, Chapter 12 dives into the landmarks along the road: those events that people remember, argue about, and carry in their identity.

When Chick-fil-A affirmed a traditional view of marriage in 2012, a chicken sandwich, for many, became a cultural symbol.[183] What felt like a market decision became a religious signal. The backlash from progressives, the mass support from conservatives, and the debates in the media all revealed how consumer identity had become theological.

---

[183] Kim Severson, "Chick-fil-A Thrust Back into the Spotlight on Gay Rights," *New York Times*, July 25, 2012, https://www.nytimes.com/2012/07/26/us/chick-fil-a-thrust-back-into-the-spotlight-on-gay-rights.html.

For many Christians, buying (or defending) a sandwich felt like an act of witness. The lines that day weren't just about appetite, they were about allegiance. Conviction turned consumer. Allegiance became appetite.

Not long after, another icon entered the spotlight. When Phil Robertson made comments critical of homosexuality and was suspended by A&E, evangelical Christians rallied behind him.[184] Robertson became a cultural hero, a sort of "outsider prophet," a man unafraid to speak God's truth even in the face of backlash.

This episode turned a duck-hunting family into a flashpoint in the culture war. It wasn't about ducks, it was about devotion. It suggested that Christian voices were marginalized and that one needed boldness to speak truth in a hostile climate. For many, the story of Duck Dynasty became a parable: faith must cost something, even social capital.

When the Supreme Court ruled in Burwell v. Hobby Lobby (2014) that closely held Christian businesses could refuse to provide contraceptives contrary to their convictions, it felt like a vindication of religious freedom.[185] This case became a landmark: faith, for the first time in many minds, was not only a private conviction but a protected public identity. The courtroom became the new pulpit, and the verdict felt like revival moment.

For many evangelicals, it confirmed that the courts, and thus political engagement, mattered deeply. The ruling underscored how law can become a battleground for religious belief, reinforcing that activism and legal strategy were part of Christian witness.

---

184 Alan Blinder and Bill Carter, "A&E Reinstates Phil Robertson," *New York Times*, December 27, 2013, https://www.nytimes.com/2013/12/28/business/media/a-e-reinstates-phil-robertson.html

185 Burwell v. Hobby Lobby Stores, Inc., 573 U.S. 682 (2014).

One of the clearest ways faith and conservatism merged was in the prophecy culture, the mixture of end-times expectation and political narrative. When politics became unpredictable, prophecy promised certainty.

Since the 1970s, books like The Late Great Planet Earth and later the Left Behind series formed a generation to read global headlines through biblical prophecy.[186]

America was often cast not just as a nation among nations, but as the bulwark of the end-of-days plan. The idea was that events in the US might be signs that the final chapters of history were falling into place.

This mindset intensified in the 2000s and 2010s. It sometimes turned ballots into battlefields and cast presidents in prophetic terms. Some prophetic voices claimed that Donald Trump was divinely appointed to resist global evil or to lead a national revival.[187]

When such prophecies failed, e.g. predictions of reelection, or timelines that didn't materialize, some believers grew disillusioned, others reinterpreted the failure, and some doubled down in assurance of deeper revelation.

A danger within prophecy culture is the risk of collapsing God's timeline into America's timeline, treating national leadership and electoral results into theological linchpins. It creates a temptation to see Jesus "behind Trump," or to conclude that failure in politics equals failure in God's plan.

---

[186] Hal Lindsey and Carole C. Carlson, *The Late Great Planet Earth* (Grand Rapids, MI: Zondervan, 1970); Tim LaHaye and Jerry B. Jenkins, *Left Behind* (Wheaton, IL: Tyndale House, 1995).

[187] Brad Christerson and Richard Flory, The Rise of Network Christianity: How Independent Leaders Are Changing the Religious Landscape (New York: Oxford University Press, 2017), 141–45.

On January 6, 2021, the US Capitol was stormed by a mob attempting to overturn the presidential election.[188] Among the crowd were Christian symbols, crosses, "Jesus Saves" signs, prayer declarations.[189] Some Christians interpreted the event as a last-stand spiritual moment, others as a dark tragedy that betrayed the gospel. For many, it felt like the Current of the Culture overflowed, faith language and fury appearing in the same streets.

For many observers, it epitomized what happens when faith and political identity fuse so tightly that violence seems like a form of worship or protest. The image of crosses in a riot became a stark symbol: when Christianity is weaponized, its witness is wounded.

In a tragic and shocking turn, conservative activist Charlie Kirk was assassinated on September 10, 2025, while speaking at a university event in Utah.[190] News outlets and social media turned the tragedy into spectacle, deepening its symbolic weight. Kirk, cofounder of Turning Point USA, was seen by many as a voice for a younger generation of conservative Christians. That a public figure so deeply entwined with Christian-conservative identity would be targeted violently has profound implications.

For some, his death was framed in prophetic language, as though a martyr had fallen in the spiritual war.

For others, it was a warning sign of how volatile the fusion of politics and faith has become.

---

188 Elizabeth Dias and Ruth Graham, "How White Evangelical Christians Fused with Trump Extremism," *New York Times*, January 11, 2021, https://www.nytimes.com/2021/01/11/us/evangelicals-capitol-mob.html.

189 Samuel L. Perry, Andrew L. Whitehead, and Joshua B. Grubbs, The Flag and the Cross: Christian Nationalism and the Threat to American Democracy (New York: Oxford University Press, 2022), 101–4.

190" Conservative Activist Charlie Kirk Killed in University Shooting," *Associated Press*, September 10, 2025.

In the weeks that followed, media and political commentary exploded. Some warned of political violence, others demanded religious symbolism be protected, others pointed fingers across party lines.

The reactions exposed how prophecy-tinged identity can edge toward sacrificial thinking: when a leader is idealized, defending him can feel like a spiritual mandate, and violence against him can be framed as a cosmic attack. It also revealed how fragile the public Christian identity is when its foundations rest on power and politics rather than on Christ. *When belief turns a leader into a savior, it forgets that salvation already came.*

Other Flashpoints in Recent Memory:

- The Tea Party movement (2009): Fiscal protest + moral revival.[191]
- Trump rallies: At times cast as revival events, with worship music, prophetic injections, and pastor endorsements.
- The COVID-19 era: Mask mandates, church closures, vaccines, all became moral litmus tests.[192] Some Christians interpreted resistance or compliance in spiritual terms, turning public health into spiritual test.
- Confederate symbols, LGBTQ+ rights, school curricula: Frequent skirmishes over what should be in textbooks, which pronouns students use, which flags fly, each debate carrying moral, spiritual, and political weight.[193]

Each moment added sediment to the same stream.

---

191 Theda Skocpol and Vanessa Williamson, The Tea Party and the Remaking of Republican Conservatism (New York: Oxford University Press, 2012), 32–38.

192 Andrew Whitehead and Samuel Perry, "Christian Nationalism, COVID-19, and the Politics of Belief," *Sociology of Religion* 83, no. 3 (2022): 302–10.

193 Kristin Kobes Du Mez, Jesus and John Wayne: How White Evangelicals Corrupted a Faith and Fractured a Nation (New York: Liveright, 2020), 245–49.

These culturally charged events don't just reflect the fusion, they educate it. Culture became a kind of catechism. They tell Christians what loyalty looks like, what bravery looks like, what betrayal looks like. For many, they become formative.

If someone first encounters conservative Christianity through a Chick-fil-A rally, a prophetic sermon about Trump, or media commentary on Jan. 6, they might come away thinking Christianity is about political commitment more than about Jesus.[194]

From fast-food counters to headline tragedies, from prophetic declarations to Capitol unrest, these touchpoints reveal how deeply political identity has shaped the American church's language and imagination.

The question that remains is urgent: Are these stories drawing people to Christ, or transforming the church into another political tribe?

Because if the narrative about Christianity is more about flags, culture wars, and failed prophecies than about the cross and resurrection, the church must ask whether we are telling a gospel or a political myth. When the gospel becomes a slogan, grace becomes a stranger.

The fusion didn't begin in a single event. It happened slowly, through trends, tone, and time. Like sediment gathering at the bottom of a river, it settled beneath the surface until the water itself changed color. Now, we can see it everywhere. Not in one scandal or sermon, but in the small compromises we've learned to call normal.

Here are four places the fusion shows itself most clearly in our culture today.

---

[194] Robert P. Jones, *The End of White Christian America* (New York: Simon & Schuster, 2016), 178–82.

1. Worship as Performance

Somewhere along the line, we stopped asking, "Did God move?" and started asking, "Did people like it?" The lights got brighter, the songs got louder, and excellence became synonymous with anointing. There's nothing wrong with skill, heaven is full of beauty, but when the stage outshines the Savior, something sacred slips away. We can learn to applaud before we learn to kneel. The applause fades; His presence remains. We can drift toward emotion over encounter, spectacle over surrender but worship was never meant to be consumed. It was meant to consume us.

The early church had no sound system, no screens, no smoke, only surrendered hearts. And that was enough to shake empires.[195]

2. Politics as Religion

In the absence of unity, ideology became our liturgy. We sometimes treat politics like a pulpit and policy like gospel. Every election cycle feels like a spiritual war, and every opponent becomes a heretic. We talk about saving America more than saving souls. We defend a nation's identity while neglecting our own in Christ. But God's Kingdom isn't in danger. It's not up for vote, and it never hangs in the balance of who sits in office. When we fuse faith too tightly with politics, we risk losing both, because the cross can't be carried in one hand while clutching control in the other.[196]

---

195 Frank Viola, Reimagining Church: Pursuing the Dream of Organic Christianity (Colorado Springs: David C. Cook, 2008), 55–59.

196 David French, Divided We Fall: America's Secession Threat and How to Restore Our Nation (New York: St. Martin's Press, 2020), 91–94.

3. Social Media as Sanctuary

The early church met in homes. We meet in comment sections. We can end up replacing fellowship with following and confession with captions. We curate what we want others to see and call it authenticity. We build platforms to promote Jesus, then quietly use Him to promote ourselves. We post verses but ignore voices. We are "connected," yet lonelier than ever. Digital discipleship has made us reactive instead of reflective. And until we learn to log off long enough to listen, the Spirit will keep competing with our scroll. The world doesn't need a viral church. It needs a faithful one.[197] The Church once gathered to break bread; now it gathers to break news.

This is a really challenging section for me. Because I have been one of the biggest voices promoting digital church, and I still fully believe in using digital tools to reach and disciple people. Digital tools are gifts; they just make terrible gods. However, when those tools become the thing that we end up worshipping, we have once again missed the mark. Digital ministry should be a bridge to tables, not a substitute for them, moving people toward tangible relationships with Jesus and His people.

4. The Self as Savior

Underneath every other fusion lies this one: the gospel of self. It's the quiet belief that I am the center, that God exists to fulfill me, not to transform me. We've redefined holiness as happiness and obedience as oppression.[198] We love the idea of Jesus the Friend but avoid Jesus the Lord. And in trying to make the gospel more palatable, we've stripped it of its power. Self-expression replaced surrender. Therapy sometimes

---

[197] Jay Y. Kim, Analog Church: Why We Need Real People, Places, and Things in the Digital Age (Downers Grove, IL: InterVarsity Press, 2020), 73–78.

[198] Carl R. Trueman, The Rise and Triumph of the Modern Self: Cultural Amnesia, Expressive Individualism, and the Road to Sexual Revolution (Wheaton, IL: Crossway, 2020), 39–45.

replaced theology. We learned to say "my truth" more than "Thy will." And in doing so, we crowned ourselves kings of kingdoms that can't save. But the cross still stands as a contradiction, not to shame us, but to save us from the weight of worshiping ourselves.

Alongside these flashpoints, there were quiet counter-stories: prayer rooms, neighborhood mercy, local revivals, moments when the church refused the script and simply loved.

But for many, the 21st-century fusion has a thousand faces, but one root: we forgot the difference between God's Kingdom and our kingdom.

Yet The River of Life still runs. Even in the confusion, God is stirring hearts that want something real again, a church without a spotlight, a faith without filters, a holiness that can't be branded.[199] Beneath the noise, there's still the sound of living water.

It starts with honesty. With repentance. With a generation willing to lose relevance to regain reverence. Because we don't need a new kind of Christianity—we just need Christ.

🕮 Reflection Questions

1. How have prophecy teachings shaped your view of politics or America's role in God's plan?
2. What cultural moment(s) have most influenced your faith identity?
3. How do you think Christians should respond when public events are interpreted as prophetic or spiritual?

---

[199] Eugene H. Peterson, A Long Obedience in the Same Direction: Discipleship in an Instant Society (Downers Grove, IL: InterVarsity Press, 2000), 23–26.

4. If a Christian leader is killed or persecuted, what should our theological response be, prophetic warfare, grief, lament, or something else?

5. What symbols (beyond flags and politics) should the church be known for in the world?

Chapter Thirteen

HATING EVIL, CLINGING TO GOOD, TRUTH IN THE GREY

Paul's words still cut through the noise of every age. In a world addicted to outrage and apathy alike, he draws a line that still divides light from shadow.

Love must be sincere. Hate what is evil; cling to what is good." Romans 12:9[200]

Few commands in Scripture are harder than this: hate what is evil, cling to what is good. Not "ignore evil." Not "tolerate it." Not "fight evil with evil." Our generation often alternates between indifference and indignation, yet struggles with imitation of Christ.[201]But hate it, and still love sincerely.

That's a razor's edge most of us don't walk well. We can fall into the ditch of moral compromise, where everything is tolerated in the name

200 Romans 12:9 (NRSV or NIV).

201 Dallas Willard, The Divine Conspiracy: Rediscovering Our Hidden Life in God (San Francisco: HarperOne, 1998), 291–95.

of love, or the ditch of moral arrogance, where everything is condemned in the name of truth.[202]

The call of Jesus is neither. It's holy love. A love with a spine. A grace that doesn't flinch. It's the kind of love that refuses to celebrate what is wicked, but also refuses to become wicked in the process of opposing it.

We live in an age that often hesitates to call evil what it is Everything feels nuanced, subjective, "based on your perspective." We are told that truth is relative and morality is personal.[203] And yet, beneath that cultural fog, people still ache for something solid, for goodness that is real and evil that is recognizable. When everything is shaded in gray, even what should be obvious can begin to look neutral.

But here's the danger: when people no longer trust institutions or faith traditions to name right and wrong, we begin to outsource morality to political tribes. Evil can drift into "whatever the other side does," and good into "whatever helps our team win"

We've seen this play out in the American church.

Some of us have confused patriotism with holiness; others, activism with righteousness. Still others have grown cynical altogether, calling everything corrupt and nothing sacred. We've sometimes wrapped the cross in our colors, and then wondered why the world sees politics before it sees Jesus.

In each case, we have exchanged biblical discernment for cultural reaction.

---

202 Timothy Keller, The Meaning of Marriage: Facing the Complexities of Commitment with the Wisdom of God (New York: Dutton, 2011), 189–93.

203 Alasdair MacIntyre, *After Virtue: A Study in Moral Theory*, 3rd ed. (Notre Dame, IN: University of Notre Dame Press, 2007), 1–5.

We're tempted to hate too quickly, or not at all.

Romans 12:9 calls us to something far deeper than slogans or sides, it calls us to discernment.

To hate what is evil means to see sin for what it really is, the corruption of something God made good. To cling to what is good means to hold fast to what reflects God's nature, even when it's costly or unpopular.

Discernment is not about picking a political team. It's about tuning our consciences to the frequency of Heaven.[204] It's about developing the eyes of Jesus, who could look at a sinner and see both the wound and the rebellion, the brokenness and the beauty.

Jesus hated evil more fiercely than anyone who ever lived, yet sinners felt safe in His presence. He never lowered the standard; He lifted the sinner. That's the paradox of holy love. He overturned tables in the temple, yet wept over the city that rejected Him.[205] He called out hypocrisy, yet restored the woman caught in adultery.

Truth in His mouth was never cruel, and grace in His heart was never weak.

It's possible to hate evil and still be consumed by it, when our hatred loses its holiness.

When we start fighting darkness with darkness, we lose the light we claim to defend.[206] The river of righteousness can't stay clear if we keep pouring rage into it. That's why Paul follows "hate what is evil" with "cling to what is good." The two are inseparable.

---

[204] Henri J. M. Nouwen, Discernment: Reading the Signs of Daily Life (New York: HarperOne, 2013), 47–52.

[205] Luke 19:41–45 (NRSV).

[206] Martin Luther King Jr., *Strength to Love* (New York: Harper & Row, 1963), 43–46.

It's not enough to condemn injustice; we must also embody justice. It's not enough to call out lies; we must also live truthfully. It's not enough to expose darkness; we must also shine light.

The moment our opposition to evil becomes fueled by rage instead of love, we're no longer contending for the kingdom of God, we're building one of our own. Rage may win arguments, but only love wins souls.

That's what happened to many reformers of the past. In their zeal to defend truth, they began to wield it more like a weapon than a witness, and at times sounded like the very Pharisees Jesus rebuked.[207]

When Jesus confronted evil, He did it differently than the world expected:

He confronted the powerful with truth, and the powerless with mercy.

He called out hypocrisy, not humanity.

He refused to be co-opted by the political movements of His day on either side, Rome or Zealots, Sadducees or Pharisees.

His Kingdom was not of this world, but it spoke powerfully into it. He showed that holiness is not separation from sinners, but transformation in their midst. That's the model we've forgotten. We've learned how to denounce sin, but not how to deliver people from it. We've learned how to argue truth, but not how to embody it. Jesus ' way was relational, not reactionary. He didn't post outrage. He knelt in dirt. He didn't call for a boycott. He called for repentance. He didn't curse His enemies. He died for them. And somehow, that was how evil was defeated.

---

[207] Richard Foster, Streams of Living Water: Celebrating the Great Traditions of Christian Faith (San Francisco: HarperOne, 1998), 112–16.

Throughout history, America has struggled to define goodness without returning to the God who defines it. Our founding ideals of liberty and justice were noble, but often selectively applied. Our story has always been a mirror, reflecting grace while revealing our blindness.

In times of moral crisis, from slavery to segregation to modern polarization, the church has faced the same test:

Will we cling to what is good, even when it costs us power?

Will we hate what is evil, even when it hides under our own flag?

The truth is, not everything that feels patriotic is automatically good, and not everything that feels progressive is automatically evil. God is neither left nor right, He is holy. Every side of a movement is capable of distorting righteousness to serve their vision of control.

Our job as followers of Jesus is not to defend a political narrative, but to discern a moral reality.

The question isn't "Is America good?" or "Is conservatism bad?"

The question is, "Does this reflect the character of Christ?"

If it does, cling to it.

If it doesn't, have the courage to call it what it is, even when that risks offending our own side.

The challenge for modern disciples isn't spotting evil in its obvious forms, violence, greed, injustice. It's recognizing it when it comes dressed in virtue.

Selfishness disguised as freedom.

Fear disguised as faithfulness.

Control disguised as conviction.

Pride disguised as patriotism.

Evil rarely introduces itself honestly. It doesn't say, "I'm here to corrupt you." It says, "I'm here to protect you." Deception seldom wears horns, it wears false halos. That's why discernment is so essential, because deception often looks like devotion.

We have to ask, not just "Is this right?" but "Is this Christlike?"

Not just "Is this effective?" but "Is this holy?"

Clinging to what is good will always come at a cost. It may cost you popularity, comfort, or even belonging within your own tribe. The Current of compromise flows more easily than the current of conviction

Jesus' goodness got Him killed.

He loved too deeply for the religious, and spoke too truthfully for the powerful.

In our time, goodness may mean standing against the tide, refusing to mock those you disagree with, speaking up for those who have no voice, or choosing integrity when compromise would be easier.

Hating evil and clinging to good may leave you misunderstood by more than one side. But that's what happens when you follow the narrow way.

Courage, in the Kingdom, doesn't look like outrage. It looks like endurance. It looks like quiet faithfulness in a noisy world. It looks like loving your enemy while refusing to excuse their sin. Kingdom courage whispers when the world shouts.

The world's courage says, "Take a stand." Jesus 'courage says, "Take up your cross."[208] The world says, "Fight until you win." Jesus says, "Love until it's finished." That kind of courage doesn't trend. It transforms.

---

[208] John Stott, *The Cross of Christ* (Downers Grove, IL: InterVarsity Press, 1986), 241–44.

Hate Evil, Love People, Cling to God. Not a slogan, it's a sequence.

In the end, Paul's command can't be obeyed apart from relationship. You can't truly hate evil unless you love people. And you can't cling to what is good unless you're clinging to God. Evil is not defeated by sharper arguments but by deeper holiness.[209] Goodness is not preserved by cultural power but by spiritual integrity. That's why the call to hate evil and cling to good isn't a political strategy; it's a discipleship path. It's not a battle plan for culture wars; it's a blueprint for Christlikeness. Revival doesn't start in the culture; it starts in the conscience.

And if the Church would live that way again, the world might finally see what truth looks like wrapped in love. The Church would move against *The Current of Culture*, and in rhythm with *The River of Life*.[210]

[209] A. W. Tozer, *The Pursuit of God* (Harrisburg, PA: Christian Publications, 1948), 97–100.

[210] Ezekiel 47:1–12; John 7:38 (NRSV).

Part

III

THE REVERSAL - LEARNING TO SWIM UPSTREAM

But every current can be resisted.

The same Spirit that carried the early church against Rome's tides still calls us today, not to escape the world, but to live differently within it.

This section invites us to rediscover the practices, priorities, and postures that align our hearts with The River of Life.

Chapter Fourteen

JESUS AND POLITICS: A DIFFERENT WAY

We've traced the river of American faith long enough to see where its current runs fast, and where it sometimes slows or gets dammed. Now we turn to the source itself, the River Jesus offers: a better flow, a better way, a current that leads to life.

When Jesus was born, His people were already asking political questions. Rome occupied Judea with soldiers, taxes, and cultural dominance. Caesar Augustus claimed to be "lord" and "savior of the world."[211] Herod the Great ruled as a client king of Rome, notorious for paranoia and brutality. Politics wasn't just a backdrop to His ministry; it was part of the water He walked in.

Every Jew lived under constant political tension. Each group had its own current, resistance, compromise, isolation, and all of them were pulling in different directions.

---

211 N. T. Wright, *Paul: A Biography* (New York: HarperOne, 2018), 53–55.

- Should we resist Rome with violence (like the Zealots)?[212]
- Should we compromise for survival (like the Sadducees)?
- Should we preserve tradition to remain pure (like the Pharisees)?
- Should we withdraw altogether (like the Essenes)?

When Jesus appeared, many wanted Him to validate their strategy. But He didn't. Instead, He declared: "The kingdom of God has come near. Repent and believe the good news!" (Mark 1:15.)[213]

This was revolutionary language. A"kingdom" meant politics, authority, and allegiance. But Jesus 'Kingdom didn't look like Rome's empire, or Israel's hopes.

Jesus refused to be trapped in the categories of His time. Consider a few key moments:

- Taxes to Caesar (Matthew 22:15–22)
    - Religious leaders tried to trap Him: "Is it right to pay the imperial tax to Caesar?" If He said no, He'd be branded a revolutionary. If yes, He'd lose credibility with His oppressed people. Jesus asked for a coin. "Whose image is on it?" "Caesar's," they said. "Render to Caesar what is Caesar's, and to God what is God's." His answer was both brilliant and disarming.[214] He acknowledged government authority without surrendering ultimate loyalty. Coins carried Caesar's image, but you carry God's. Give Caesar his coin, but give God your heart.

---

212 Scot McKnight, The King Jesus Gospel: The Original Good News Revisited (Grand Rapids, MI: Zondervan, 2011), 31–36.

213 Mark 1:15 (NRSV).

214 Matthew 22:15–22 (NRSV).

- Before Pilate (John 18:36)
  - On trial, Pilate asked if He was a king. Jesus replied: "My kingdom is not of this world. If it were, my servants would fight."[215] His Kingdom wasn't advanced by swords or soldiers, but by truth, love, and sacrifice. His words still challenge every empire tempted to baptize its power.
- The Triumphal Entry (Matthew 21:1–11)
  - Crowds expected a military messiah, riding in like a conqueror. Jesus entered Jerusalem on a donkey, a symbol of humility, not war.[216] His Kingdom challenged their expectations.
- The Sermon on the Mount (Matthew 5–7)
  - If Rome's empire was built on power, and Israel's leaders sought control, Jesus taught:
  - Blessed are the poor in spirit.
  - Love your enemies.
  - Turn the other cheek.
  - Do not worry about tomorrow.
  - It was a constitution for a Kingdom not built on control, but on character, the politics of purity, mercy, and peace.[217]

It was a kind of manifesto for an upside-down Kingdom.

After the resurrection, the early church lived under Caesar's shadow. How did they navigate politics?

---

[215] John 18:36 (NRSV).

[216] Matthew 21:1–11 (NRSV); see Zechariah 9:9.

[217] Stanley Hauerwas, *The Peaceable Kingdom: A Primer in Christian Ethics* (Notre Dame, IN: University of Notre Dame Press, 1983), 64–70.

Paul in Romans 13 said to honor governing authorities, but always within the greater framework of God's Kingdom.

Peter in 1 Peter 2:17 said: "Honor everyone. Love the brotherhood. Fear God. Honor the emperor." The emperor who persecuted Christians was still to be respected, but never worshiped.

Acts 5:29 shows the boundary line: "We must obey God rather than men."[218]

The early church didn't launch a political party. They couldn't lobby Caesar; instead, they lived faithfully, caring for widows, rescuing abandoned babies, feeding the hungry. Their radical love made Rome take notice. By the 4th century, parts of the empire began to be transformed.[219] Instead of damming the current, they let grace flow freely through acts of mercy and justice.

At the center of Jesus 'engagement with politics is the cross. If Rome ruled through fear, Jesus ruled through forgiveness. Rome used crucifixion to humiliate rebels and crush resistance. It was the empire's symbol of power. [220]

But Jesus turned it upside down. On the cross, He displayed:

- Power through weakness. He could have called angels but chose surrender.
- Victory through sacrifice. He triumphed not by killing but by dying.
- Authority through love. He forgave His executioners.

---

218 Acts 5:29 (NRSV).

219 Peter Brown, The Rise of Western Christendom: Triumph and Diversity, AD 200–1000, 10th anniv. ed. (Oxford: Blackwell, 2013), 67–71.

220 Martin Hengel, Crucifixion in the Ancient World and the Folly of the Message of the Cross (Philadelphia: Fortress Press, 1977), 22–27.

The cross revealed that the Kingdom of God advances not by coercion but by compassion, not by domination but by dying to self.

This "politics of the cross" stands in sharp contrast with the fusion of conservatism and Christianity in America:

- Earthly politics seeks power. Jesus models servanthood (Mark 10:42–45).[221]
- Earthly kingdoms build thrones; Jesus carried a cross.
- Partisanship divides. Jesus unites Jew and Gentile, slave and free, male and female (Galatians 3:28).
- Ideologies idolize nations. Jesus said His Kingdom is not of this world.
- Propaganda thrives on fear. Jesus repeatedly said: "Do not be afraid."[222]

Whenever the church forgets this, it risks replacing discipleship with ideology. We start baptizing platforms instead of people.

So what does it look like to practice Jesus 'politics in the 21st century?

- Kingdom Citizenship First
    - Philippians 3:20 reminds us: "Our citizenship is in heaven."[223] This doesn't mean withdrawing from earthly life; it means everything else is secondary. Party loyalty, national identity, even cultural values cannot define us more than Christ does. Citizens of Heaven are called to swim upstream, not in defiance, but in devotion

[221] Mark 10:42–45 (NRSV); see John Howard Yoder, *The Politics of Jesus*, 2nd ed. (Grand Rapids, MI: Eerdmans, 1994), 33–39.
[222] Luke 12:32; Matthew 14:27 (NRSV).
[223] Philippians 3:20 (NRSV); see Michael Gorman, Cruciformity: Paul's Narrative Spirituality of the Cross (Grand Rapids, MI: Eerdmans, 2001), 284–88.

- Truth and Love Together
    - Jesus came "full of grace and truth" (John 1:14).[224] Modern politics often forces a choice: be harshly truthful or endlessly tolerant. The way of Jesus is both, conviction without cruelty, compassion without compromise.
- Servanthood Over Power
    - In politics, greatness is measured by influence and control. In the Kingdom, greatness is measured by service. Christians are called to wash feet, not win battles.[225] The greatest revolutions in history have been carried in calloused hands, not clenched fists.
- Prophetic, Not Partisan
    - The prophets of Israel critiqued every king, calling them to justice and righteousness.[226] Christians today are wise to resist becoming chaplains to any party. Our role is to hold all sides accountable to God's standards. Prophets speak truth to every throne; partisans often echo the ones that favor them.

Modern Examples of Kingdom Witness:

- Martin Luther King Jr. led a civil rights movement rooted in biblical justice and nonviolence.[227] He confronted power, but always with love.

---

224 John 1:14 (NRSV).

225 John 13:12–15 (NRSV).

226 Amos 5:24; Micah 6:8 (NRSV); Walter Brueggemann, *The Prophetic Imagination*, 2nd ed. (Minneapolis: Fortress Press, 2001), 56–60.

227 Martin Luther King Jr., Letter from Birmingham Jail, April 16, 1963.

- Dietrich Bonhoeffer resisted Hitler not by baptizing German nationalism but by holding fast to Christ, even to martyrdom.[228]
- The persecuted church worldwide often has no political power, yet its faithful witness has spread the gospel in places of oppression. Believers in underground churches across China or Iran understand this better than most; their faith thrives not because of freedom, but because of faithfulness.[229]

These examples show what happens when believers live as citizens of Christ's Kingdom first.

If we're honest, many of us in the American church have struggled to follow this way. At times, we've sought Caesar's power more than Christ's cross. We've traded prophetic voice for political influence. We traded the flowing river for a moat of self-preservation. We've allowed fear of losing a nation to overshadow faith in the One who holds every nation.[230] But Jesus invites us back. Back to the river where surrender is strength, and where peace runs deeper than politics. Back to the Kingdom that is not shaken by elections. Back to the gospel that is good news for all nations. Back to the cross, where true power is revealed.

The Kingdom of Jesus isn't apolitical, it's more transformative than any politics this world has ever seen[231] But it is political not through domination, but through love; not through coercion, but through grace; not through fear, but through hope.

---

228 Dietrich Bonhoeffer, *Ethics*, ed. Eberhard Bethge (New York: Macmillan, 1965), 149–53.

229 David Aikman, Jesus in Beijing: How Christianity Is Transforming China and Changing the Global Balance of Power (Washington, DC: Regnery Publishing, 2003), 245–47.

230 Isaiah 40:15–17 (NRSV).

231 Oliver O'Donovan, The Desire of the Nations: Rediscovering the Roots of Political Theology (Cambridge: Cambridge University Press, 1996), 15–19.

In a polarized America, the church has a chance to show something radically different. Not left. Not right. But a people living under a King whose throne is a cross and whose law is love.[232] The River of His Kingdom still flows, not red or blue, but crimson, carrying life to all who step in.

🕮 REFLECTION QUESTIONS

1. Which group in Jesus 'time do you most identify with (Zealots, Pharisees, Sadducees, Essenes)? Why?
2. How does the Sermon on the Mount challenge the way you think about politics?
3. What does it mean to practice the "politics of the cross" in your community?
4. Who today models Kingdom citizenship more than partisan loyalty?
5. How might the American church repent and reorient itself toward this better way?

---

232 Philippians 2:5–11 (NRSV).

Chapter Fifteen

AMERICA, BLESS GOD, REVERSING THE PRAYER THAT SHAPED A NATION

Few phrases stir the American heart like 'God bless America. [233]' It echoes through stadiums, floats over fireworks, and lingers in living rooms after tragedy. It unites people across party lines and generations. It feels both reverent and patriotic, a humble appeal for divine favor.

Over time, though, those three words began to take on a different tone. They shifted from a prayer of dependence to a declaration of entitlement. From "Lord, have mercy" to something closer to "Lord, keep us comfortable." The prayer became a slogan; the dependence became demand.[234]

At times, we've treated God's blessing like a birthright instead of a responsibility, like something He owed us because of our history, our prosperity, or our moral superiority.

---

[233] Irving Berlin, *God Bless America*, song (1938; New York: Irving Berlin Inc.).

[234] Robert Bellah et al., Habits of the Heart: Individualism and Commitment in American Life (Berkeley: University of California Press, 1985), 221–26.

Scripture rarely commands nations to seek blessings for themselves.[235] It commands them to bless God through obedience, justice, and humility. And that's the reversal our hearts desperately need: Not "God bless America," but "America, bless God."

When the early settlers spoke of God's blessing, it was in the language of covenant, not comfort. They saw blessing as the fruit of faithfulness, not a guarantee of power.[236]

But over time, especially after the Revolution and during westward expansion, "blessing" became synonymous with success. The American Dream often overshadowed the Kingdom of God as our vision of flourishing.[237]

We stopped measuring blessing by holiness, and started measuring it by GDP. We turned stewardship into statistics. We sometimes stopped seeking God's face, and started using His name to defend our way of life. And so, our national prayer drifted from gratitude to assumption, from "God, make us faithful," to "God, keep us favored."

To bless God is to acknowledge His worth and respond with worship, obedience, and gratitude. It's not about asking Him to serve our plans, but surrendering our plans to His purposes. It's not asking God to orbit our nation; it's choosing to revolve our nation around God.

When Scripture says "Bless the Lord, O my soul" (Psalm 103:1), it doesn't mean we add something to God's greatness.[238] It means we recognize it. It's a posture of reverence, a heart turned upward rather than inward.

---

235 Deuteronomy 8:10–20; Psalm 33:12 (NRSV).

236 Perry Miller, *Errand into the Wilderness* (Cambridge, MA: Harvard University Press, 1956), 56–60.

237 James K. A. Smith, Desiring the Kingdom: Worship, Worldview, and Cultural Formation (Grand Rapids, MI: Baker Academic, 2009), 53–58.

238 Psalm 103:1 (NRSV); see Walter Brueggemann, Israel's Praise: Doxology against Idolatry and Ideology (Minneapolis: Fortress Press, 1988), 17–20.

So what would it mean for a nation to bless God? Imagine a nation whose strength was measured by mercy, whose heroes were servants, whose greatness was gratitude. It would mean our laws reflect His justice. Our leaders seek His wisdom, not just their polls. Our churches would care more about the poor than about preserving influence. Our people value righteousness over comfort. It would mean gratitude that leads to generosity, and freedom that leads to faithfulness. A nation blesses God not with words, but with the way it treats His image-bearers.[239]

Idolatry is when we take something good and treat it as ultimate. It's what happens when the current of blessing flows inward instead of outward. When we sing "God bless America" yet neglect repentance or justice, we aren't blessing God; we're asking Him to bless our idol. When we ask God to bless our nation's prosperity but ignore the poor, to bless our freedom but overlook the enslaved, to bless our military but forget the peacemakers, we're praying for favor without transformation. That's not worship, it's misunderstanding.[240]

The prophet Amos said it plainly: "I hate your religious festivals; your assemblies are a stench to me But let justice roll on like a river, righteousness like a never-failing stream." (Amos 5:21–24.) God's river struggles to flow through polluted worship.

God doesn't bless pride. He blesses repentance.

He doesn't favor nations that exalt themselves. He draws near to those that humble themselves.

America's founding ideals, liberty, justice, equality, are not unbiblical. In fact, they echo the language of the gospel. But ideals become idols when we pursue them apart from God's character. They were echoes of Eden, but without obedience, even echoes fade.

---

239 Matthew 25:31–40 (NRSV).

240 Isaiah 1:11–17 (NRSV); see Amos 5:21–24.

Freedom without holiness becomes chaos. Prosperity without generosity becomes greed.

Power without humility becomes tyranny. The call of the Church in America is not to abandon love of country, it's to purify it. To remind the nation that the truest blessing is not comfort or success, but character.

When freedom is used to serve others, it blesses God.

When justice is pursued even when it costs us, it blesses God.

When truth is spoken even against our tribe, it blesses God.

When worship is more than a lyric at a baseball game, it blesses God.

Blessing God isn't a lyric; it's a lifestyle.

Scripture gives us example after example of what happens when a people mistake divine blessing for divine approval.

Israel prospered under David and Solomon, but when they began to trust in wealth and weapons, prophets like Isaiah and Jeremiah warned that their blessing would vanish if they forgot the Lord.[241] Every empire thinks it's the exception, until its blessings run dry.

Rome once tolerated Christians, then persecuted them, then adopted them, and in doing so, merged empire and faith until the cross became a political emblem instead of a symbol of sacrifice.[242]

Modern America has followed a similar pattern: gratitude turned to presumption, humility to hubris. Blessing begins to crumble when it leads to self-sufficiency. We mistake God's patience for His approval.

---

241 1 Kings 10–11; Isaiah 31:1 (NRSV).

242 Peter Leithart, Defending Constantine: The Twilight of an Empire and the Dawn of Christendom (Downers Grove, IL: InterVarsity Press, 2010), 33–39.

The prayer "God bless America" is not wrong, but it is incomplete if it never leads us to say, "Lord, teach us to bless You in return."[243]

When Jesus was asked about greatness, He said, "The greatest among you will be your servant." (Matthew 23:11)[244] Greatness in God's eyes has always looked upside down to the world. That's the heart of a nation that truly blesses God, not one obsessed with being first, but one devoted to being faithful. The question is not, "Will America stay great?" The question is, "Will America stay grateful?"

If we lose gratitude, we lose perspective. If we lose humility, we lose blessing.[245]

God's kingdom does not rise or fall with any one nation.[246] But nations rise or fall with how they respond to His kingdom.

A nation blesses God when:

- Justice is more than a slogan.
- Truth matters more than winning.
- Compassion crosses party lines.
- Churches repent before they protest.
- Leaders serve before they seek power.

A nation blesses God when its justice rolls, its mercy flows, and its heart beats in rhythm with The River of Life.

In other words, a nation blesses God when it looks like the Sermon on the Mount more than the shouting of a campaign rally. When mercy triumphs over judgment, when peacemakers are honored more than pundits, when we care less about restoring our own greatness and more

243 Psalm 67:1–2 (NRSV).
244 Matthew 23:11 (NRSV).
245 Luke 14:11 (NRSV).
246 Daniel 2:21; Psalm 22:28 (NRSV).

about making Jesus known again, that's when a nation begins to bless God.

It's not too late to flip the prayer. Every revival begins with a reversal, when we stop treating God as the mascot of our politics and start honoring Him as the Lord of our lives. To say: "Lord, You have blessed us beyond measure, now teach us to bless You back." That shift changes everything. It turns nationalism into gratitude. It turns pride into worship. It turns fear into faith.

When a people learn to bless God, they rediscover who they are: not chosen because of merit, but called because of mercy. The river of repentance always leads to renewal, but it must first pass through surrender.

In Ezekiel, the river flowed from the temple. In Christ, the river flows from Himself, He is the living temple (John 7:37–39). And now, we are the temple (1 Corinthians 6:19).[247] That means the same river now flows through us. The River of Life flows from within you, not because of you, but because of Him. The River is still flowing. Its strength has not weakened, only our willingness to step in. So may America stop asking for blessing, and start becoming one.

So we "bless God" when we allow that current of life to actually make a difference in the way we make decisions, interact with others, and flee from idols. To follow Him means swimming against the polluted currents of this world. It means resisting comfort, conformity, and control. It means moving in the opposite direction, toward holiness, truth, and love. You can't drift toward holiness; you have to swim toward it.[248]

---

[247] Ezekiel 47:1–12; John 7:37–39; 1 Corinthians 6:19 (NRSV).

[248] Hebrews 12:14; Philippians 3:12–14 (NRSV).

Chapter Sixteen

DISCIPLES BEFORE VOTERS: PRACTICAL STEPS FOR TODAY'S CHURCH

The story of conservatism and Christianity in America is not just a history lesson. It reveals something deeper: much of the church's political captivity has often been a discipleship problem.[249] It's a mirror. One that reflects what happens when formation gives way to fusion.

When believers know more about their party's platform than Jesus' Sermon on the Mount, we've replaced discipleship with ideology.[250] When our churches talk more about elections than the resurrection, we've confused the Kingdom of God with the kingdoms of men. When we can quote our favorite pundits more easily than the prophets, it's a sign we're drifting.

Recovering our witness in the 21st century means re-centering our lives around Christ, not politics. We are disciples first, voters second. Only

[249] Dallas Willard, The Great Omission: Reclaiming Jesus's Essential Teachings on Discipleship (San Francisco: HarperSanFrancisco, 2006), 17–20.
[250] Matthew 5–7 (NRSV).

then can the current of the Kingdom cut through the chaos of our culture.[251]

If we are to swim against the current, the Church must make five deliberate turns.

1. From Partisan Identity → Kingdom Identity

Political parties are temporary; the Kingdom is eternal. Churches must teach believers to hold their political identity lightly and their Kingdom identity firmly. That means: preaching Jesus, not parties; celebrating baptism more than election victories.

Reminding people that their truest passport is Philippians 3:20: "Our citizenship is in heaven."[252] You can't carry a cross well if your hands are too full of flags

2. From Consuming Media → Meditating on Scripture

Many Christians spend hours a day consuming partisan media but only minutes a week in the Word. No wonder our voices sometimes echo pundits more than prophets. Formation happens by repetition. The question isn't whether you're being formed, but by what.[253]

A simple rule: before you scroll, let Scripture speak. This small shift could re-train hearts to see the world through God's lens.

---

[251] John 18:36; Romans 14:17 (NRSV).

[252] Philippians 3:20 (NRSV); see Michael J. Gorman, Cruciformity: Paul's Narrative Spirituality of the Cross (Grand Rapids, MI: Eerdmans, 2001), 284–88.

[253] James K. A. Smith, You Are What You Love: The Spiritual Power of Habit (Grand Rapids, MI: Brazos Press, 2016), 25–28.

3. From Fear-Driven Politics → Hope-Filled Witness

Much of modern faith-and-politics fusion, across the spectrum, has been fueled by fear: fear of losing America, fear of cultural change, fear of being marginalized. But fear is never a biblical motivator. Fear shrinks the gospel to survival. Hope expands it to resurrection.[254]

Jesus constantly said: "Do not be afraid." The early church thrived not because they clung to influence but because they radiated hope in Christ.[255]

Practical step: when we speak about politics, we must ask: are we fueling fear, or pointing people to hope?

4. From Winning Culture Wars → Serving a Broken World

The church has sometimes acted as though it could save the nation by winning arguments, passing laws, or boycotting companies. But Jesus ' strategy was different: "The Son of Man came not to be served but to serve."[256] The cross was not a conquest, it was compassion displayed.

Practical step: Instead of rallying only for political causes, what if churches rallied around radical service? Feeding the hungry, mentoring kids in foster care, standing with the marginalized.[257] These are political acts too, just in a Kingdom way. These are currents of the Kingdom, quiet, but unstoppable.

---

254 2 Timothy 1:7; Romans 15:13 (NRSV).

255 Alan Kreider, The Patient Ferment of the Early Church: The Improbable Rise of Christianity in the Roman Empire (Grand Rapids, MI: Baker Academic, 2016), 47–52.

256 Mark 10:45 (NRSV).

257 Matthew 25:35–40 (NRSV).

5. From Political Power → Prophetic Presence

The prophets of Israel spoke truth to kings, but they never became pawns of kings.[258] In our time, the church must recover its prophetic role, not cheerleading parties, but challenging all parties in light of God's justice, mercy, and truth. The Church doesn't need the king's throne when it already serves the King of Kings.

Practical step: pastors and churches should measure their success not by access to politicians but by faithfulness to proclaiming the whole counsel of God, even when it offends their own political tribe.

With no political leverage, the first Christians cared for the sick during plagues, adopted abandoned babies, and treated slaves as family. Their witness changed the Roman Empire, not through legislation but through love. Their credibility came not from control, but from compassion.

MLK modeled a faith-rooted political engagement that confronted injustice without being co-opted by partisanship. His nonviolent resistance was profoundly political, but it was also profoundly Christian. He reminded America that justice is never partisan, it's prophetic.

In places like China or Iran, Christians have no political voice.[259] Yet their witness is powerful because their allegiance to Christ is clear. They remind us that faith flourishes even without political dominance.

If reformation begins anywhere, it begins in the rhythms of ordinary believers.

---

258 Amos 5:24; Micah 6:8 (NRSV); Walter Brueggemann, *The Prophetic Imagination*, 2nd ed. (Minneapolis: Fortress Press, 2001), 56–60.

259 David Aikman, Jesus in Beijing: How Christianity Is Transforming China and Changing the Global Balance of Power (Washington, DC: Regnery Publishing, 2003), 245–47.

Practical Guidance for Individuals:

- Vote, but don't worship. Participate in democracy, but remember no candidate is the Messiah.[260]
- Engage issues, not just parties. Ask what Scripture says about life, justice, creation, family, and then apply it consistently. The cross doesn't fit neatly into any column.
- Seek diverse voices. Listen to Christians across political lines to avoid echo chambers. Truth has nothing to fear from tension.
- Practice spiritual disciplines. Fasting, prayer, Sabbath, and Scripture guard us against being discipled by media.[261]
- Be peacemakers online. Social media disciples us toward outrage; Christians can disrupt that with gentleness and truth. The comment section is today's public square, let's make it holy ground.

Practical Guidance for Churches:

- Preach the whole gospel. Don't shrink the good news to one set of issues. Preach Jesus as Lord over all of life.[262] If Jesus is Lord of all, then no issue is off-limits, but no issue replaces Him.
- Create spaces for dialogue. Small groups where people with different political views can listen and pray together. Discipleship grows in circles, not just rows.
- Focus on formation. Teach practices of prayer, service, generosity, and Scripture to re-center identity in Christ.

---

260 John 18:36; Psalm 146:3 (NRSV).

261 Richard J. Foster, *Celebration of Discipline: The Path to Spiritual Growth*, rev. ed. (San Francisco: HarperSanFrancisco, 1998), 13–16.

262 Colossians 1:17–18 (NRSV).

- Reject manipulation. Don't let your pulpit become a campaign rally. Let's not outsource discipleship to cable news or social media.[263] Every pulpit that trades truth for access loses both.
- Lift up global Christianity. Remind people the church is bigger than America, and God's Kingdom is flourishing worldwide.[264] Perspective breaks pride.

The Bible often describes God's people as exiles, citizens of heaven living faithfully in a foreign land. Like Daniel in Babylon, or the early church in Rome, we are called not to seize power but to bear faithful witness.[265] Exiles don't dam The River of Life, they keep it flowing, faithfully, until the Kingdom comes.

In America, that means voting and engaging with wisdom, but remembering that the Church's mission is not to save a nation. It's to embody and announce the reign of Jesus. Faithful presence is greater than political dominance.[266]

If we can recover that vision, perhaps the next generation won't see Christians mainly as angry partisans, but as people of peace, hope, and radical love. People who stopped fighting *The Current of Culture* long enough to flow with *The River of Life*.[267]

---

263 John Stott, Between Two Worlds: The Challenge of Preaching Today (Grand Rapids, MI: Eerdmans, 1982), 98–100.

264 Philip Jenkins, The Next Christendom: The Coming of Global Christianity, 3rd ed. (Oxford: Oxford University Press, 2011), 6–9.

265 Daniel 6:10; Acts 4:19–20 (NRSV).

266 James Davison Hunter, To Change the World: The Irony, Tragedy, and Possibility of Christianity in the Late Modern World (Oxford: Oxford University Press, 2010), 244–46.

267 Ezekiel 47:1–12; John 7:38 (NRSV).

🕮 Reflection Questions

1. In what ways have you been discipled more by politics than by Jesus?
2. Which of the five shifts (identity, Scripture, hope, service, prophecy) do you most need to embrace?
3. How could your church model the politics of the Kingdom in your community?
4. What would it look like to live as an "exile" in America, faithful to Christ but not captive to parties?

Chapter Seventeen

RHYTHMS FOR FAITHFUL ENGAGEMENT

Here's the truth: no one drifts into discipleship. We're all being shaped by a current, the only question is, which one?[268]

If we run with the metaphors of the currents, we are either being formed by the current of this world, or the current that flows out of the Spirit of God. Both have pull, both promise freedom, but only one leads to life. Regardless, something is forming and shaping us.

Discipleship is not neutral. If we don't intentionally form our lives around Christ, we will be formed by something else.[269] And in our cultural moment, politics is one of the most powerful forces shaping hearts

Every push notification, podcast, or headline is a tiny act of discipleship. It teaches us what to fear, who to hate, and where to place our hope. Without counter-rhythms, Christians will slowly (or quickly)

---

[268] Romans 12:2 (NRSV); James K. A. Smith, You Are What You Love: The Spiritual Power of Habit (Grand Rapids, MI: Brazos Press, 2016), 25–28.

[269] Dallas Willard, The Spirit of the Disciplines: Understanding How God Changes Lives (New York: Harper & Row, 1988), xii–xiv.

become more conformed to Fox News or MSNBC than to Jesus Christ. Each swipe is a subtle sermon, each scroll a small surrender.[270]

Rhythms, what Christians throughout history have called a Rule of Life.[271] A Rule of Life isn't a cage; it's a trellis for growth. They give us structure so that the vine of our faith can flourish in a chaotic environment. They anchor us so we aren't swept away by the current of noise.[272]

This chapter gives us practices you can actually do, as individuals, families, or churches. Because if formation is the current, practice is how we swim.

These rhythms are small acts of resistance, tiny oars paddling against the cultural tide.

Daily Rhythms

1. Scripture Before Screens

Why it matters: Political media forms us through fear and outrage. Scripture forms us through truth and hope.

Practice: Before you touch your phone in the morning, read one chapter of Scripture. Start with the Psalms or the Gospels.[273]

Counter-formation: Instead of being discipled by headlines, you are discipled by God's Word.

Reflection Prayer:"Lord, let Your Word be the loudest voice in my life today."

---

270 Alan Noble, You Are Not Your Own: Belonging to God in an Inhuman World (Downers Grove, IL: InterVarsity Press, 2021), 87–91.

271 St. Benedict, *The Rule of St. Benedict*, trans. Timothy Fry (Collegeville, MN: Liturgical Press, 1981), Prologue 45–50.

272 John 15:4–5 (NRSV).

273 Psalm 1:1–3; Joshua 1:8 (NRSV).

Formation begins in the first five minutes of your day.

2. Prayer for Leaders and Enemies

Why it matters: Politics divides the world into winners and losers; prayer reminds us we're all beggars before grace.

Practice: Each day, pray for one leader you voted for and one you didn't. Then pray for an "enemy," someone whose politics offend you.

Counter-formation: This turns outrage into intercession and rehumanizes people politics wants us to despise.

Reflection Prayer:

"Father, bless and guide those I disagree with. Form in me the heart of Christ, who prayed for His enemies."

3. Practicing Silence

Why it matters: The political machine runs on noise. God often speaks in whispers. In silence, we remember who is actually running the world.

Practice: Take 10 minutes daily for silence before God. No phone, no news, no agenda.

Counter-formation: Silence trains us to resist being constantly reactive.

Reflection Prayer:

"Speak, Lord, for Your servant is listening."

Weekly rhythms slow us down enough to remember who we are.

Weekly Rhythms

4. Fasting From Media

Why it matters: Media overload distorts our vision of reality. A break resets our perspective. What we consume consumes us.

Practice: Choose one day a week to fast from all political news and social media.

Counter-formation: Fasting reminds us that truth doesn't live in pundits, it lives in Christ.

Reflection Prayer:

"Lord, quiet the noise of the world so I can hear Your voice."

5. Sabbath Rest

Why it matters: Sabbath resists the idols of control, productivity, and fear. The River of Life still flows while we rest, because it's His current, not ours.

Practice: Once a week, turn off the news and stop striving. Enjoy God, family, and creation.

Counter-formation: Sabbath reminds us God sustains the world, not us, not our nation.

Reflection Prayer:

"Lord, I rest in You. The government is on Your shoulders, not mine."

6. Hospitality to the Other

Why it matters: Political tribes isolate us. Jesus broke bread with Pharisees, tax collectors, and Samaritans. Every shared table is a protest against tribalism.

Practice: Once a week, share a meal or coffee with someone outside your political bubble. Ask more questions than you answer.

Counter-formation: Hospitality builds empathy in a culture of suspicion.

Reflection Prayer:

"Lord, teach me to see Your image in those who think differently from me."

Monthly rhythms widen the circle, moving us from personal formation to communal transformation.

Monthly Rhythms

7. Service in the Community

Why it matters: Politics tempts us to fight for abstract issues. Service keeps us grounded in real people. You can't love your neighbor abstractly; you have to show up.

Practice: Once a month, serve outside your church, at a shelter, food bank, or prison.

Counter-formation: Instead of just talking about justice, you embody it.

Reflection Prayer:

"Jesus, let me see Your face in the least of these."

8. Corporate Confession

Why it matters: Politics thrives on blaming others. Confession reminds us to start with our own sins. Before revival begins in the streets, it begins in confession at the altar.

Practice: Once a month, confess as a church, our pride, idolatry, fear, and compromise.

Counter-formation: Confession humbles us, breaking the cycle of tribal arrogance.

Reflection Prayer:

"Lord, have mercy on me, a sinner. Have mercy on us, Your church."

Yearly rhythms remind us of the long obedience in the same direction.

Yearly Rhythms

9. ELECTION PRACTICES

Why it matters: Elections are the high tide of political discipleship. Without counter-rhythms, they overwhelm us. Voting becomes worship when it's done in surrender, not self-importance.

Practices:

Fast from partisan media during debates.

Read the Gospels during campaign season.

Pray before you vote: "I give this ballot to Caesar, but my heart belongs to You."

Counter-formation: This reframes voting not as worship of a nation, but as stewardship under God.

10. GLOBAL AWARENESS

Why it matters: The Kingdom is global. Politics shrinks our vision to national borders. Seeing the global church keeps our river from becoming a stagnant pond.

Practice: Once a year, spend intentional time learning from the global church, reading stories, giving, or even visiting.

Counter-formation: Global awareness humbles us, reminding us God's plan is bigger than America.

Putting It Together: A Sample "Rule of Life"

Think of it as a rhythm map for swimming upstream.

- Daily – Scripture before screens, prayer for leaders, silence.
- Weekly – Media fast, Sabbath, hospitality.

- Monthly – Service, confession.
- Yearly – Election practices, global awareness.

This is not about adding more tasks. It's about re-training our souls so that we aren't discipled by the outrage of culture, but by the peace of Christ.[274]

These rhythms are not apolitical. They are deeply political because they shape us into a people who live differently in the world. They resist the false gods of partisanship, nationalism, and fear, and re-form us into the image of Christ. They are the politics of the Kingdom, the kind that flow, not fight.[275]

If practiced widely, these rhythms could change the church's public witness. Imagine a people known less for angry debates and more for silence, prayer, service, and hospitality. Imagine a church marked not by fear of losing power but by hope in a crucified and risen King.[276] That's the kind of politics Jesus calls us to practice.

That's the current of life we were meant to swim in.

And if the Church learns these rhythms again, perhaps the world will finally see *The River of Life* for what it is—a stream of grace wide enough for all to enter.[277]

🕮 REFLECTION QUESTIONS

1. Which of these rhythms would most change your political posture if you practiced it faithfully?
2. What barriers keep you from adopting a Rule of Life like this?

---

[274] Colossians 3:15–16 (NRSV).
[275] Ezekiel 47:1–12; John 7:38 (NRSV).
[276] 1 Peter 1:3–4 (NRSV).
[277] John 12:32; Isaiah 55:1 (NRSV).

3. How might your church embody these rhythms together in the next election season?

4. What's one step you can take this week to begin living as a disciple before a voter?

Part IV
THE RENEWAL

The river hasn't run dry. It still flows from the throne of God, inviting weary travelers to step in once again.

Renewal begins not in the halls of power, but in the hearts of disciples who choose the narrow way.

These closing chapters remind us that hope isn't found in reclaiming control, but in reclaiming our first love.

Chapter Eighteen

RECLAIMING THE KINGDOM WITNESS: HOPE FOR THE FUTURE

The story of American Christianity is not just about politics, although I know I have spent a lot of time on that in this book. It's about identity, discipleship, and witness. Politics may have captured our headlines, but identity has always been the deeper story. At times, the Church has been known more for its partisan loyalties than for the gospel of Jesus.

The result?

- Generations walking away from the church, not because of Jesus, but because they cannot see Him apart from politics. They are not rejecting Jesus, they're walking away from a Jesus they can no longer see through the fog of politics.[278]
- A reputation shaped more by fear, anger, and outrage than by love, joy, and peace.[279]
- A witness that has been compromised at the very moment the world most needs clarity.

[278] David Kinnaman and Gabe Lyons, unChristian: What a New Generation Really Thinks About Christianity... and Why It Matters (Grand Rapids, MI: Baker Books, 2007), 25–28.

[279] Galatians 5:22–23 (NRSV).

But crisis is also opportunity. The moments when the church has been most tempted to chase power are also the moments when God has invited us back to the cross. Every shaking becomes a sifting, revealing what is built on the Rock and what is built on sand.[280]

The American church is not the first to face these challenges. Throughout history, God's people have been tempted to trust earthly kings instead of the King of Kings.[281] But God has always raised up a remnant, a people who refuse to bow to idols, who live faithfully in the shadow of empires. Every empire has a river of compromise running through it, but God always preserves a current of faithfulness.[282]

- In Babylon, Daniel and his friends stood firm without violence, proving God's power was greater than the king's.[283]
- In Rome, the early Christians transformed the empire not with armies, but with hospitality, service, and witness.[284]
- In the civil rights era, men and women of faith showed the world what nonviolent love could do against the machinery of injustice.[285]

The same Spirit who empowered them is at work in us.

---

[280] Matthew 7:24–27; Hebrews 12:26–27 (NRSV).

[281] 1 Samuel 8:4–7 (NRSV).

[282] Daniel 1:8; Revelation 14:4 (NRSV).

[283] Daniel 3:16–18; Daniel 6:10 (NRSV).

[284] Rodney Stark, The Rise of Christianity: How the Obscure, Marginal Jesus Movement Became the Dominant Religious Force in the Western World (San Francisco: HarperSanFrancisco, 1996), 82–87.

[285] Martin Luther King Jr., Letter from Birmingham Jail, April 16, 1963.

If we want to reclaim the church's credibility and influence, not as a voting bloc but as a faithful presence, then we must:

- **Return to Jesus as Lord.**
    - Not America. Not a party. Not a candidate. Not a cause. Only Christ.[286]
- **Practice the politics of the Kingdom.**
    - Servanthood instead of domination. Hope instead of fear. Love instead of outrage.[287]
- **Adopt rhythms of resistance.**
    - Daily, weekly, monthly, and yearly practices that re-train us to live as disciples first.
- **Tell a better story.**
    - Rather than culture war narratives, the church must tell the gospel story: creation, fall, redemption, restoration. That story is bigger than America's story and offers hope for the nations.[288]

Imagine if the next generation knew Christians not as angry culture warriors, not as the loudest voices in the room, but as the quiet streams that bring life wherever they flow.

- People who serve their neighbors radically.
- People who pray faithfully for leaders they agree with and those they don't.

---

286 Philippians 2:9–11; Colossians 1:15–18 (NRSV).

287 Mark 10:42–45; John 13:12–15 (NRSV).

288 N. T. Wright, Simply Christian: Why Christianity Makes Sense (New York: HarperOne, 2006), 33–37.

- People who are not addicted to outrage but anchored in peace.[289]
- People who welcome the stranger, care for the poor, and defend the vulnerable.[290]
- People whose lives point unmistakably to Jesus.

This is possible. But it requires courage to disentangle our faith from partisan captivity and rediscover our true calling.

One of the most humbling reminders is that the church is not American, it's global. Christianity is growing fastest in Africa, Latin America, and Asia.[291] The American church is not the center of God's Kingdom, but one expression among many. Our faith was born in the deserts of the Middle East, refined in the catacombs of Rome, and now thrives in places the news rarely mentions.

If we lift our eyes, we see a future where:

- The global church reminds us that persecution does not destroy faith, it refines it.[292]
- Younger believers in America hunger for authenticity, not partisanship.[293]
- The Spirit is already at work, stirring movements of prayer, justice, and evangelism outside the echo chambers of politics.
- The Kingdom is advancing, with or without our political influence.[294]

The final question is not, "Can America be saved?" but "Will the church be faithful?"

---

289 Philippians 4:6–7 (NRSV).
290 Matthew 25:35–40; James 1:27 (NRSV).
291 Philip Jenkins, The Next Christendom: The Coming of Global Christianity, 3rd ed. (Oxford: Oxford University Press, 2011), 6–9.
292 Tertullian, *Apologeticus*, 50.13; see also Revelation 2:10 (NRSV).
293 Barna Group, *Reviving Evangelism* (Ventura, CA: Barna Group, 2019), 22–25.
294 Matthew 16:18; Daniel 2:44 (NRSV).

Jesus is not wringing His hands over Congress or the Supreme Court. His throne is secure.[295] His gospel is unstoppable. His Spirit is alive in His people. He's still walking on the waters we're afraid to step into.

The invitation is simple, but costly:

- To repent of idolatry.
- To re-center on Christ.
- To live as disciples first, voters second.
- To reclaim a witness that looks like Jesus in a world desperate to see Him.

That's why the writer of Hebrews reminds us where our true stability lies. Hebrews 12:28 says: "Therefore, since we are receiving a kingdom that cannot be shaken, let us be thankful, and so worship God acceptably with reverence and awe."[296]

Nations will rise and fall. Parties will come and go. America itself is not eternal. But the Kingdom of God will never be shaken. Empires erode, but *The River of Life* keeps flowing.[297]

This is our hope. This is our identity. This is our future.

And if the church in America can reclaim this vision, then maybe, just maybe, our children and grandchildren will not remember us as the people who fused faith with politics, but as the people who lived and loved like Jesus in a divided world.[298]

---

[295] Psalm 2:1–6; Revelation 19:6 (NRSV).
[296] Hebrews 12:28 (NRSV).
[297] Ezekiel 47:1–12; Revelation 22:1–2 (NRSV).
[298] John 13:34–35 (NRSV).

🕮 REFLECTION QUESTIONS

1. What idols has the American church been tempted to bow to in politics?
2. What practices give you hope that the church can reclaim its witness?
3. What does it mean for you personally to be a "disciple before a voter"?
4. How can your community embody a Kingdom that cannot be shaken?

Chapter Nineteen

A PERSONAL WORD OF HOPE

I've written this book with both a heavy heart and a hopeful one. Heavy, because I've seen firsthand how *The Current of Culture*, this fusion of politics and faith, has divided churches, fractured families, and clouded the witness of Christ. Hopeful, because I believe the gospel still shines brighter than any headline, and the Kingdom of God still stands taller than any empire.[299] We can still choose which water to step in! *The Current of Culture*, or *The River of Life.*

Maybe as you've read, you've felt the sting of conviction, or the quiet ache of realization. Maybe you've recognized ways that your own faith has been entangled with politics. If so, you're not alone. I've felt it too. All of us, in one way or another, have been discipled more by the noise of the world than by the still small voice of the Spirit.[300]

But here's the good news: Jesus doesn't shame us; He invites us. Not with condemnation, but with compassion.[301] His Kingdom is open to

---

299 Daniel 2:44; Matthew 6:33 (NRSV).
300 1 Kings 19:11–12; John Mark Comer, *The Ruthless Elimination of Hurry* (Colorado Springs, CO: WaterBrook, 2019), 45–47.
301 John 3:17; Matthew 11:28–30 (NRSV).

every weary partisan, every burned-out activist, every believer who feels torn in two. His way is still the better way.

The challenges aren't going away. America will stay polarized. Elections will get uglier. Social media will stay loud. Culture wars will keep raging. The storms aren't slowing down. But anchors only prove worth in rough waters.[302]

But the church doesn't have to play by those rules. We don't have to be tossed back and forth by fear, outrage, or tribalism. We can be a people who live differently, anchored in Christ, practicing rhythms of discipleship, and showing the world a Kingdom that cannot be shaken.[303]

Imagine the witness of a church that is known more for washing feet than winning debates.[304] A church that is quicker to pray than to post. A church that carries crosses, not flags.[305] A church that is not defined by the pundits it follows but by the Savior it adores. Imagine the sound, not of shouting crowds, but of running water as the Church bends low again.

That church can change the world.

My Prayer for You

If you've made it this far, thank you. You've wrestled with history, with culture, with Scripture, and with the challenge of what it means to follow Jesus in America today.

Every one of us is in a current. The question isn't whether you're being carried; it's which way you're going. Some stand safely on the shore. Some wade in ankle-deep. Some fight the current. And some have

---

302 Hebrews 6:19 (NRSV).
303 Romans 12:2; Hebrews 12:28 (NRSV).
304 John 13:12–15; Philippians 2:3–5 (NRSV).
305 Luke 24:27, 32 (NRSV).

finally let go, fully immersed in the river that flows from God's throne.[306]

The currents of this world are polluted and easy to follow. The current of the Kingdom is pure, but it takes surrender.[307] The River of Life always flows against the polluted currents of the world.

My prayer for you is simple:

- That you would have the boldness to go against the current.
- That you would be a disciple first, a voter second.
- That your life would tell the story of Jesus more than the story of a party.
- That your community would embody rhythms that resist fear and outrage.
- That your eyes would stay fixed on the Kingdom that cannot be shaken.
- That one day, when people look back on our generation, they won't remember us as the church that bowed to the culture, but as the church that returned to Jesus.
- That you would set up rhythms in your life that draw you close to Jesus, not the flow of culture.

The world doesn't need another partisan movement. It needs the people of God, alive to the Spirit, grounded in the Word, and shaped by the cross.[308]

That's our calling. That's our hope. That's our future.

---

306 Ezekiel 47:1–9; Revelation 22:1–2 (NRSV).
307 Romans 12:2; James 4:7–8 (NRSV).
308 Acts 1:8; Romans 8:14; 1 Corinthians 2:2 (NRSV).

So let us go, not as Republicans or Democrats, not as culture warriors or cynics, but as ambassadors of Christ, citizens of heaven, servants of the Kingdom, witnesses of the gospel.[309]

Because in the end, America will pass away. But Jesus will not.[310] Every river eventually meets the sea, but this one flows into eternity.[311]

And His Kingdom is the one we truly long for.

" Come, Lord Jesus." (Revelation 22:20)[312]

The River of Life still flows. Step in.[313]

---

309 2 Corinthians 5:20; Philippians 3:20; Acts 1:8 (NRSV).
310 Matthew 24:35; Revelation 11:15 (NRSV).
311 Revelation 22:1–5 (NRSV).
312 Revelation 22:20 (NRSV).
313 Ezekiel 47:6; John 7:38 (NRSV).

BIBLIOGRAPHY

Adams, John. The Letters of John and Abigail Adams. Edited by Frank Shuffelton. New York: Penguin Classics, 2004.

,,,. The Works of John Adams. Edited by Charles Francis Adams. 10 vols. Boston: Little, Brown and Company, 1850–56.

,,,. "Thoughts on Government." 1776.

Adams, John. "To the Officers of the First Brigade of the Third Division of the Militia of Massachusetts." October 11, 1798. In The Works of John Adams, edited by Charles Francis Adams, vol. 9, 229. Boston: Little, Brown, and Company, 1854.

Addams, Jane. Twenty Years at Hull-House. New York: Macmillan, 1910.

Ahlberg Calhoun, Adele. Spiritual Disciplines Handbook: Practices That Transform Us. 2nd ed. Downers Grove, IL: InterVarsity Press, 2015.

Aikman, David. Jesus in Beijing: How Christianity Is Transforming China and Changing the Global Balance of Power. Washington, DC: Regnery Publishing, 2003.

Allitt, Patrick. The Conservatives: Ideas and Personalities Throughout American History. New Haven: Yale University Press, 2009.

Associated Press. "Conservative Activist Charlie Kirk Killed in University Shooting." September 10, 2025.

Augustine. Confessions. Translated by Henry Chadwick. Oxford: Oxford University Press, 1991.

Bailyn, Bernard. The Ideological Origins of the American Revolution. Cambridge, MA: Harvard University Press, 1967.

Barna Group. Reviving Evangelism. Ventura, CA: Barna Group, 2019.

,,,. "The State of the Church 2023." Accessed October 2025. https://www.barna.com/research/state-of-the-church-2023.

Basler, Roy P., ed. Collected Works of Abraham Lincoln. 9 vols. New Brunswick, NJ: Rutgers University Press, 1953–55.

Beck, Richard. We Believe the Children: A Moral Panic in the 1980s. New York: PublicAffairs, 2015.

Bellah, Robert N. "Civil Religion in America." Daedalus 96, no. 1 (1967): 1–21.

Bellah, Robert N., Richard Madsen, William M. Sullivan, Ann Swidler, and Steven M. Tipton. Habits of the Heart: Individualism and Commitment in American Life. Berkeley: University of California Press, 1985. (2008 ed. cited in text.)

Berlin, Irving. God Bless America. Song. New York: Irving Berlin Inc., 1938.

Berkin, Carol. A Brilliant Solution: Inventing the American Constitution. New York: Harcourt, 2002.

Bettenson, Henry, and Chris Maunder, eds. Documents of the Christian Church. 3rd ed. Oxford: Oxford University Press, 1999.

Blinder, Alan, and Bill Carter. "A&E Reinstates Phil Robertson." New York Times, December 27, 2013. https://www.nytimes.com/2013/12/28/business/media/a-e-reinstates-phil-robertson.html.

Bogaski, George. "American Protestants and the Debate over the Vietnam War." The Christian Century, October 29, 2014. https://www.christiancentury.org/reviews/2014-10/american-protestants-and-debate-over-vietnam-war-george-bogaski

Bonhoeffer, Dietrich. Ethics. Edited by Eberhard Bethge. New York: Macmillan, 1965.

,,,. The Cost of Discipleship. New York: Macmillan, 1959.

Boyer, Paul. When Time Shall Be No More: Prophecy Belief in Modern American Culture. Cambridge, MA: Harvard University Press, 1992.

Brewer, David J. Church of the Holy Trinity v. United States, 143 U.S. 457 (1892).

Brown, Peter. The Rise of Western Christendom: Triumph and Diversity, A.D. 200–1000. 2nd ed. Oxford: Blackwell, 2003.

,,,. The Rise of Western Christendom: Triumph and Diversity, A.D. 200–1000. 10th anniv. ed. Oxford: Blackwell, 2013.

Brooks, David. The Second Mountain: The Quest for a Moral Life. New York: Random House, 2019.

Bugliosi, Vincent, and Curt Gentry. Helter Skelter: The True Story of the Manson Murders. New York: W. W. Norton, 1974.

Bush, George W. Decision Points. New York: Crown, 2010.

,,,. "Address to a Joint Session of Congress and the American People." September 20, 2001. The American Presidency

Project. Accessed October 2025. https://www.presidency.ucsb.edu.

Byrd, Daniel K., and Jonathan H. Ebel, eds. Faith and War: How Christians Debated the Cold and Vietnam Wars. New York: New York University Press, 2016. https://www.universitypressscholarship.com/view/10.18574/nyu/9780814741337.001.0001/upso-9780814741337

Ceplair, Larry. The Public Years of Sarah and Angelina Grimké. New York: Columbia University Press, 1989.

Chappell, David L. A Stone of Hope: Prophetic Religion and the Death of Jim Crow. Chapel Hill: University of North Carolina Press, 2004.

Cohen, Lizabeth. A Consumers 'Republic: The Politics of Mass Consumption in Postwar America. New York: Vintage, 2003.

Cohen, Stanley. Folk Devils and Moral Panics. London: Routledge, 1972.

Congressional Record. House of Representatives. 100th Cong., 2nd sess. (1954): 8618.

Constitution of the United States of America. 1787.

De Tocqueville, Alexis. Democracy in America. 2 vols. New York: Vintage Classics, 1990.

"Declaration of Independence: A Transcription." National Archives. July 4, 1776. https://www.archives.gov/founding-docs/declaration-transcript.

Dobbs v. Jackson Women's Health Organization, 597 U.S. 215 (2022).

Douglass, Frederick. Narrative of the Life of Frederick Douglass, an American Slave. Boston: Anti-Slavery Office, 1845.

Du Mez, Kristin Kobes. Jesus and John Wayne: How White Evangelicals Corrupted a Faith and Fractured a Nation. New York: Liveright, 2020.

Durkheim, Émile. The Division of Labor in Society. Translated by George Simpson. New York: Free Press, 1933.

Ebel, Jonathan. Faith in the Fight: Religion and the American Soldier in the Great War. Princeton, NJ: Princeton University Press, 2010.

"Edict of Milan" (313 CE). In Henry Bettenson and Chris Maunder, eds., Documents of the Christian Church, 22–23. Oxford: Oxford University Press, 1999.

"Edict of Thessalonica" (380 CE). In Henry Bettenson and Chris Maunder, eds., Documents of the Christian Church, 24–25. Oxford: Oxford University Press, 1999.

Eisenhower, Dwight D. "Inaugural Address." January 20, 1953. In Public Papers of the Presidents of the United States. Washington, DC: GPO, 1953.

Ellul, Jacques. The Technological Society. Translated by John Wilkinson. New York: Vintage, 1964.

Encyclopaedia Britannica. "Meeting of Waters." Last modified July 3, 2024. https://www.britannica.com/place/Meeting-of-Waters.

Engel v. Vitale, 370 U.S. 421 (1962).

Eskridge, Larry. God's Forever Family: The Jesus People Movement in America. New York: Oxford University Press, 2013.

Esch, Jennifer. "How Christian Political Factions Influenced America During the Vietnam War." Michigan Journal of History (2014). https://michiganjournalhistory.wordpress.com/wp-content/uploads/2014/02/esch_jennifer.pdf

Escoffier, Jeffrey. Sexual Revolution. New York: Oxford University Press, 2003.

Eusebius of Caesarea. Ecclesiastical History and Life of Constantine.

,,,. Life of Constantine. Book I, ch. 28. New York: Christian Classics Ethereal Library, 1890 trans.

Farber, David. The Age of Great Dreams: America in the 1960s. New York: Hill and Wang, 1994.

FitzGerald, Frances. The Evangelicals: The Struggle to Shape America. New York: Simon & Schuster, 2017.

Foner, Eric. Reconstruction: America's Unfinished Revolution, 1863–1877. New York: Harper & Row, 1988.

Foster, Richard J. Celebration of Discipline: The Path to Spiritual Growth. Rev. ed. San Francisco: HarperSanFrancisco, 1998.

Foster, Richard. Streams of Living Water: Celebrating the Great Traditions of Christian Faith. San Francisco: HarperOne, 1998.

French, David. Divided We Fall: America's Secession Threat and How to Restore Our Nation. New York: St. Martin's Press, 2020.

Gaddis, John Lewis. The Cold War: A New History. New York: Penguin Press, 2005.

Gay, Peter. The Enlightenment: An Interpretation, Vol. 1: The Rise of Modern Paganism. New York: Knopf, 1966.

Gerson, Michael. "The Last Temptation." The Atlantic, April 2018. https://www.theatlantic.com.

Gorman, Michael J. Cruciformity: Paul's Narrative Spirituality of the Cross. Grand Rapids, MI: Eerdmans, 2001.

Graham Library Archives. "Ronald Reagan and Evangelical Support." Accessed October 15, 2025. https://billygrahamlibrary.org.

Guiley, Rosemary. The Encyclopedia of Demons and Demonology. New York: Facts On File, 2009.

Haeg, Sarah. "Catholicism and the Anti–Vietnam War." Honors thesis, College of Saint Benedict and Saint John's University, 2018. https://digitalcommons.csbsju.edu/cgi/viewcontent.cgi?article=1059&context=honors_thesis

Haidt, Jonathan. The Righteous Mind: Why Good People Are Divided by Politics and Religion. New York: Vintage Books, 2013.

Hamilton, Alexander. The Federalist Papers. Edited by Clinton Rossiter. New York: Signet Classics, 2003.

,,,. "The Federalist No. 70." In The Federalist Papers, 423–24. New York: Signet Classics, 2003.

Hardman, Susan Friend. Faith and Freedom: Jerry Falwell and the Rise of the Religious Right. Chapel Hill: University of North Carolina Press, 1987.

Hatch, Nathan O. The Democratization of American Christianity. New Haven: Yale University Press, 1989.

Hauerwas, Stanley. The Peaceable Kingdom: A Primer in Christian Ethics. Notre Dame, IN: University of Notre Dame Press, 1983.

Hengel, Martin. Crucifixion in the Ancient World and the Folly of the Message of the Cross. Philadelphia: Fortress Press, 1977.

Hickam Jr., Homer H. Rocket Boys: A Memoir. New York: Delacorte Press, 1998.

Hunter, James Davison. To Change the World: The Irony, Tragedy, and Possibility of Christianity in the Late Modern World. Oxford: Oxford University Press, 2010.

Jackson, Andrew. "Second Annual Message to Congress." December 6, 1830. In The Papers of Andrew Jackson, vol. 8, edited by Daniel Feller et al., 245–48. Knoxville: University of Tennessee Press, 2010.

Jenkins, Philip. The Next Christendom: The Coming of Global Christianity. 3rd ed. New York: Oxford University Press, 2011.

Jones, Robert P. The End of White Christian America. New York: Simon & Schuster, 2016.

,,,. White Too Long: The Legacy of White Supremacy in American Christianity. New York: Simon & Schuster, 2020.

Kant, Immanuel. "What Is Enlightenment?" (1784). In Practical Philosophy, edited and translated by Mary J. Gregor, 11–12. Cambridge: Cambridge University Press, 1996.

Keller, Timothy. The Meaning of Marriage: Facing the Complexities of Commitment with the Wisdom of God. New York: Dutton, 2011.

Kidd, Thomas. Who Is an Evangelical? The History of a Movement in Crisis. New Haven: Yale University Press, 2019.

Kim, Jay Y. Analog Church: Why We Need Real People, Places, and Things in the Digital Age. Downers Grove, IL: InterVarsity Press, 2020.

Kinnaman, David, and Gabe Lyons. unChristian: What a New Generation Really Thinks About Christianity... and Why It Matters. Grand Rapids, MI: Baker Books, 2007.

Kirk, Russell. The Conservative Mind: From Burke to Eliot. 7th ed. Chicago: Regnery Books, 1986.

Kruse, Kevin M. One Nation Under God: How Corporate America Invented Christian America. New York: Basic Books, 2015.

LaHaye, Tim, and Jerry B. Jenkins. Left Behind. Wheaton, IL: Tyndale House, 1995.

Lang, Michael. The Road to Woodstock. New York: Ecco, 2009.

Larson, Edward J. Summer for the Gods: The Scopes Trial and America's Continuing Debate over Science and Religion. Cambridge, MA: Harvard University Press, 1997.

Lactantius. On the Deaths of the Persecutors. 313 CE.

Leithart, Peter. Defending Constantine: The Twilight of an Empire and the Dawn of Christendom. Downers Grove, IL: InterVarsity Press, 2010.

Lelwica, Michelle M. Shameful Bodies: Religion and the Culture of Physical Improvement. New York: Bloomsbury Academic, 2017.

Lewis, C. S. The Screwtape Letters. New York: HarperOne, 2015 (orig. 1942).

Lewisohn, Mark. The Beatles: All These Years, Vol. 1 – Tune In. New York: Crown Archetype, 2013.

Lindsey, Hal, and Carole C. Carlson. The Late Great Planet Earth. Grand Rapids, MI: Zondervan, 1970.

Locke, John. Two Treatises of Government. London: Awnsham Churchill, 1689.

Manseau, Peter. "Why Thomas Jefferson Created His Own Bible." Smithsonian Magazine, September 8, 2020.

https://www.smithsonianmag.com/history/why-thomas-jefferson-created-his-own-bible-180975343/.

Marsden, George M. Fundamentalism and American Culture: The Shaping of Twentieth-Century Evangelicalism 1870–1925. 2nd ed. New York: Oxford University Press, 2006.

Martin, William. A Prophet with Honor: The Billy Graham Story. New York: William Morrow, 1991.

,,,. With God on Our Side: The Rise of the Religious Right in America. New York: Broadway Books, 1996.

McFarland, Sean. "How American Christians Responded to the Vietnam War." Undergraduate thesis, Taylor University, 2023. https://pillars.taylor.edu/cgi/viewcontent.cgi?article=1003&context=history

Miller, Perry. Errand into the Wilderness. Cambridge, MA: Harvard University Press, 1956.

Mislin, David. "How Vietnam War Protests Accelerated the Rise of the Christian Right." Smithsonian Magazine, May 3, 2018. https://www.smithsonianmag.com/history/how-vietnam-war-protests-spurred-rise-christian-right-180968942/

Morgan, Edmund S. The Puritan Dilemma: The Story of John Winthrop. Boston: Little, Brown and Company, 1958.

National Archives and Records Administration. Records of the U.S. House of Representatives (re: Public Law 84-140).

Noll, Mark A. A History of Christianity in the United States and Canada. Grand Rapids, MI: Eerdmans, 1992.

,,,. America's God: From Jonathan Edwards to Abraham Lincoln. New York: Oxford University Press, 2002.

,,,. The Civil War as a Theological Crisis. Chapel Hill: University of North Carolina Press, 2006.

Noll, Mark A., and George Marsden. Evangelicals and Civic Life: Public Religion in America. New York: Oxford University Press, 2019.

Nouwen, Henri J. M. Discernment: Reading the Signs of Daily Life. New York: HarperOne, 2013.

Nouwen, Henri. The Way of the Heart: Connecting with God through Prayer, Wisdom, and Silence. New York: HarperOne, 1981.

O'Donovan, Oliver. The Desire of the Nations: Rediscovering the Roots of Political Theology. Cambridge: Cambridge University Press, 1996.

Old South Meeting House. "Boston Tea Party History." Accessed October 15, 2025. https://oldsouthmeetinghouse.org/history/boston-tea-party/.

Oregon Public Broadcasting. "Social media is shattering America's understanding of Charlie Kirk's death." September 20, 2025.

O'Sullivan, John L. "Annexation." United States Magazine and Democratic Review 17 (July–August 1845): 5–10.

Paine, Thomas. Common Sense. Philadelphia, 1776.

Paul Revere Heritage Site / National Park Service. "The Battles of Lexington and Concord." Accessed October 15, 2025. https://www.nps.gov/mima/learn/historyculture/the-battle-of-lexington-and-concord.htm.

Perry, Samuel L., Andrew L. Whitehead, and Joshua B. Grubbs. The Flag and the Cross: Christian Nationalism and the Threat to

American Democracy. New York: Oxford University Press, 2022.

Peterson, Eugene H. A Long Obedience in the Same Direction: Discipleship in an Instant Society. Downers Grove, IL: InterVarsity Press, 2000.

Poole, Robert. Earthrise: How Man First Saw the Earth. New Haven, CT: Yale University Press, 2008.

Postman, Neil. Technopoly: The Surrender of Culture to Technology. New York: Knopf, 1992.

Proceedings of the Southern Baptist Convention. 1863. Richmond, VA: H. K. Ellyson, 1863.

Public Law 83-396. July 14, 1954.

Public Law 84-140. July 30, 1956.

Raboteau, Albert J. Slave Religion: The "Invisible Institution" in the Antebellum South. New York: Oxford University Press, 1978.

Reagan, Ronald. "Acceptance Address at the Republican National Convention." July 17, 1980. In Public Papers of the Presidents of the United States. Washington, DC: GPO, 1980.

„,. "Evil Empire Speech." March 8, 1983. In Public Papers of the Presidents of the United States. Washington, DC: GPO, 1983.

„,. "Farewell Address to the Nation." January 11, 1989. In Public Papers of the Presidents of the United States. Washington, DC: GPO, 1989.

Reed, Ralph. Active Faith: How Christians Are Changing the Soul of American Politics. New York: Free Press, 1996.

Religion News Service. "The Vietnam Years: How the Conflict Ripped the Nation's Religious Fabric." Religion News Service, September 8, 2017. https://religionnews.com/2017/09/08/the-vietnam-years-how-the-conflict-ripped-the-nations-religious-fabric/

Reuters. "U.S. revokes visas for six foreigners over comments made about Charlie Kirk's death." October 14, 2025. https://www.reuters.com.

"Roman Religion: Cult of the Emperors." Encyclopaedia Britannica. Accessed October 15, 2025. https://www.britannica.com/topic/Roman-religion.

Roe v. Wade, 410 U.S. 113 (1973).

Root, Andrew. Faith Formation in a Secular Age. Grand Rapids, MI: Baker Academic, 2017.

Saunt, Claudio. Unworthy Republic: The Dispossession of Native Americans and the Road to Indian Territory. New York: W. W. Norton, 2020.

Sandeen, Ernest. The Roots of Fundamentalism: British and American Millenarianism, 1800–1930. Chicago: University of Chicago Press, 1970.

Schrecker, Ellen. Many Are the Crimes: McCarthyism in America. Boston: Little, Brown, 1998.

Schultz, Kevin M. Tri-Faith America: How Catholics and Jews Held Postwar Pluralism Together. New York: Oxford University Press, 2011.

Severson, Kim. "Chick-fil-A Thrust Back into the Spotlight on Gay Rights." New York Times, July 25, 2012.

https://www.nytimes.com/2012/07/26/us/chick-fil-a-thrust-back-into-the-spotlight-on-gay-rights.html.

Shaw, Robert E. American Patriotic Protestantism: National Faith and Manifest Destiny, 1800–1860. New York: Garland Publishing, 1985.

Sheils, William L., ed. The Churches, Ireland and the Irish. Oxford: Oxford University Press, 1989.

Skocpol, Theda, and Vanessa Williamson. The Tea Party and the Remaking of Republican Conservatism. New York: Oxford University Press, 2012.

Smith, James K. A. Desiring the Kingdom: Worship, Worldview, and Cultural Formation. Grand Rapids, MI: Baker Academic, 2009.

,,,. You Are What You Love: The Spiritual Power of Habit. Grand Rapids, MI: Brazos Press, 2016.

Smulyan, Susan. Selling Radio: The Commercialization of American Broadcasting, 1920–1934. Washington, DC: Smithsonian Institution Press, 1994.

Stark, Rodney. The Rise of Christianity. San Francisco: HarperSanFrancisco, 1996.

Stott, John. Between Two Worlds: The Challenge of Preaching Today. Grand Rapids, MI: Eerdmans, 1982.

,,,. The Cross of Christ. Downers Grove, IL: InterVarsity Press, 1986.

Stringfellow, Thornton. A Scriptural View of Slavery. Richmond: J. W. Randolph, 1856.

Stout, Harry S. The Divine Drummer: Jonathan Edwards and the Great Awakening. Grand Rapids, MI: Eerdmans, 1991.

,,,. Upon the Altar of the Nation: A Moral History of the Civil War. New York: Viking, 2006.

Sutton, Matthew Avery. Aimee Semple McPherson and the Resurrection of Christian America. Cambridge, MA: Harvard University Press, 2007.

Taylor, Alan. American Revolutions: A Continental History, 1750–1804. New York: W. W. Norton & Company, 2016.

"The Battles of Saratoga." Encyclopaedia Britannica. Accessed October 15, 2025.

"The Biblical Basis for and Against the Vietnam War." Times of Israel Blogs, June 15, 2025. https://blogs.timesofisrael.com/the-biblical-basis-for-and-against-the-vietnam-war/

The Freedom Trail Foundation. "History of the Freedom Trail." Accessed October 15, 2025. https://www.thefreedomtrail.org.

The Gospel Coalition. "Ken Burns 'The Vietnam War Is Worth Your Time." The Gospel Coalition, September 25, 2017. https://www.thegospelcoalition.org/article/ken-burns-the-vietnam-war-is-worth-your-time/

The Guardian. "Trump posthumously awards Charlie Kirk the Presidential Medal of Freedom." October 14, 2025. https://www.theguardian.com.

The World's Most Famous Court Trial: Tennessee Evolution Case. Cincinnati: National Book Company, 1925.

Thornton, Robert W. Torrey. Billy Sunday: The Man and His Message. Philadelphia: Sunday School Times Company, 1914.

Tocqueville, Alexis de. Democracy in America. Translated by Harvey C. Mansfield and Delba Winthrop. Chicago: University of Chicago Press, 2000.

Treaty of Paris, 1783. U.S. Treaty Series No. 80, Article I.

Trueman, Carl R. The Rise and Triumph of the Modern Self: Cultural Amnesia, Expressive Individualism, and the Road to Sexual Revolution. Wheaton, IL: Crossway, 2020.

U.S. Congress. Public Law 83-396. July 14, 1954.

U.S. Congress. Public Law 84-140. July 30, 1956.

U.S. Constitution. Article I; Article VI; Preamble.

U.S. Supreme Court. Burwell v. Hobby Lobby Stores, Inc., 573 U.S. 682 (2014).

,,,. Church of the Holy Trinity v. United States, 143 U.S. 457 (1892).

,,,. Dobbs v. Jackson Women's Health Organization, 597 U.S. 215 (2022).

,,,. Engel v. Vitale, 370 U.S. 421 (1962).

,,,. Obergefell v. Hodges, 576 U.S. 644 (2015).

Victor, Jeffrey S. Satanic Panic: The Creation of a Contemporary Legend. Chicago: Open Court, 1993.

"Vietnam War and Seventh-day Adventists." Encyclopedia of Seventh-day Adventists, May 10, 2022. https://encyclopedia.adventist.org/article?id=7AYL

Waldstreicher, David. Slavery's Constitution: From Revolution to Ratification. New York: Hill and Wang, 2009.

Warren, Rick. The Purpose Driven Church: Growth Without Compromising Your Message and Mission. Grand Rapids, MI: Zondervan, 1995.

Wells, David F. No Place for Truth: Or Whatever Happened to Evangelical Theology? Grand Rapids, MI: Eerdmans, 1993.

Whitehead, Andrew, and Samuel L. Perry. "Christian Nationalism, COVID-19, and the Politics of Belief." Sociology of Religion 83, no. 3 (2022): 302–10.

Wiencek, Henry. Master of the Mountain: Thomas Jefferson and His Slaves. New York: Farrar, Straus and Giroux, 2012.

Wigger, John. American Saint: Francis Asbury and the Methodist Movement. New York: Oxford University Press, 2009.

Wiebe, Robert H. The Search for Order, 1877–1920. New York: Hill and Wang, 1967.

Williams, Daniel K. God's Own Party: The Making of the Christian Right. New York: Oxford University Press, 2010.

Willard, Dallas. The Divine Conspiracy: Rediscovering Our Hidden Life in God. San Francisco: HarperOne, 1998.

,,,. The Great Omission: Reclaiming Jesus's Essential Teachings on Discipleship. San Francisco: HarperSanFrancisco, 2006.

,,,. The Spirit of the Disciplines: Understanding How God Changes Lives. New York: Harper & Row, 1988.

Wilson, Woodrow. "Address to Congress Requesting a Declaration of War Against Germany." April 2, 1917. Congressional Record, 65th Cong., 1st sess. (1917): 224–25.

Winthrop, John. "A Model of Christian Charity." 1630. In Collections of the Massachusetts Historical Society, 3rd ser., vol. 7, 31–48. Boston: Charles C. Little and James Brown, 1838.deu0

Wright, N. T. Paul: A Biography. New York: HarperOne, 2018.

,,,. Simply Christian: Why Christianity Makes Sense. New York: HarperOne, 2006.

Yancey, Philip. Vanishing Grace: What Ever Happened to the Good News? Grand Rapids, MI: Zondervan, 2014.

,,,. What's So Amazing About Grace? Grand Rapids, MI: Zondervan, 1997.

Yoder, John Howard. The Politics of Jesus. 2nd ed. Grand Rapids, MI: Eerdmans, 1994.

"Ancient Rome: Cult of the Emperors." Encyclopaedia Britannica. Accessed October 15, 2025. https://www.britannica.com/topic/Roman-religion.

"Battles of Saratoga." Encyclopaedia Britannica. Accessed October 15, 2025.

"History of the Freedom Trail." The Freedom Trail Foundation. Accessed October 15, 2025. https://www.thefreedomtrail.org.

"Moral Majority." Encyclopaedia Britannica. Accessed October 15, 2025. https://www.britannica.com/topic/Moral-Majority.

Oregon Public Broadcasting. "Social media is shattering America's understanding of Charlie Kirk's death." September 20, 2025.

Reuters. "U.S. revokes visas for six foreigners over comments made about Charlie Kirk's death." October 14, 2025. https://www.reuters.com.

The Guardian. "Trump posthumously awards Charlie Kirk the Presidential Medal of Freedom." October 14, 2025. https://www.theguardian.com.

Founding Documents and Statutes

Articles of Confederation. 1781.

Treaty of Paris, 1783. U.S. Treaty Series No. 80, Article I.

U.S. Congress. Public Law 83-396. July 14, 1954.

U.S. Congress. Public Law 84-140. July 30, 1956.

U.S. Constitution. Preamble; Article I; Article VI.

ABOUT KHARIS PUBLISHING

Kharis Publishing, an imprint of Kharis Media LLC, is a leading Christian and inspirational book publisher based in Aurora, Chicago metropolitan area, Illinois. Kharis' dual mission is to give voice to under-represented writers (including women and first-time authors) and equip orphans in developing countries with literacy tools. That is why, for each book sold, the publisher channels some of the proceeds into providing books and computers for orphanages in developing countries so that these kids may learn to read, dream, and grow. For a limited time, Kharis Publishing is accepting unsolicited queries for nonfiction (Christian, self-help, memoirs, business, health and wellness) from qualified leaders, professionals, pastors, and ministers. Learn more at: https://kharispublishing.com/